WINNING WAYS

WINNING

A Photohistory of
American Women in Sports

by SUE MACY

WAYS

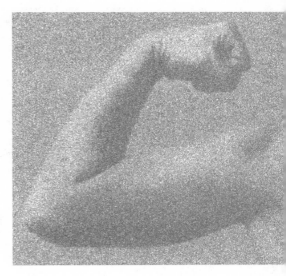

HENRY HOLT AND COMPANY   **NEW YORK**

For my parents, Ruth and Morris Macy

Henry Holt and Company, Inc.
Publishers since 1866
115 West 18th Street
New York, New York 10011

Henry Holt is a registered
trademark of Henry Holt and Company, Inc.

Published in Canada by Fitzhenry & Whiteside Ltd.,
195 Allstate Parkway, Markham, Ontario L3R 4T8.

Library of Congress Cataloging-in-Publication Data
Macy, Sue.
Winning ways: a photohistory of American women in sports / by Sue Macy.
p.   cm.
Includes bibliographical references and index.
1. Sports for women—United States—History.   2. Women athletes—
United States—History.   3. Sports for women—United States—
History—Pictorial works.   4. Women athletes—United States—
History—Pictorial works.   I. Title.
GV709. 18. U6M33   1996   796'.0194—dc20   95-44969

ISBN 0-8050-4147-8
First Edition—1996

Printed in the United States of America
on acid-free paper. ∞
10 9 8 7 6 5 4 3

CONTENTS

Author's Note
3

Acknowledgments
6

Foreword: *Raising the Banner*
10

The 1800s: *A Century of Progress*
15

1900–1919: *Pathfinders*
33

1920–1929: *The Golden Age of Sports*
51

1930–1945: *All-American Girls*
78

1946–1965: *Ladies Through and Through*
99

1966–1981: *A New Era*
125

1982–Today: *Taut, Toned, and Coming On Strong*
151

The Power and the Promise
178

Chronology: *Firsts, Records, and Other Noteworthy Events*
189

Resources
202

Index
208

WINNING WAYS

AUTHOR'S NOTE

Every so often I find a photograph that makes me look at history in a whole new way. While doing research for this book, I came across a snapshot showing the legendary Amelia Earhart, the hero of my youth, standing next to superstar athlete Babe Didrikson. Two of the most powerful, most independent women of their day, caught together by an unknown photographer while they were taking target practice with a pistol and a bow and arrow of all things. I stared at the photo for what seemed like hours, comparing the two women, trying to guess what they talked about, how they related to one another, whether they felt a bond. Finally I could almost imagine that I was there with them, just outside the camera's range.

Photographs can be powerful tools in exploring the past. Each of the photos in this book tells its own story. Some capture athletes in motion—jumping, pitching, running, punching. Others record historic meetings or historic moments. Still others catch successful athletes

3

Two of the most celebrated women of the 1930s get together for some target practice. Aviator Amelia Earhart, *left,* was on the very short list of people Babe Didrikson admired, though Babe, *right,* didn't know her well. *Photograph from the Babe Didrikson Zaharias Collection, Special Collections Department, Mary and John Gray Library, Lamar University, Beaumont, Texas*

beaming with pride. Whether they illustrate the people and events discussed in the text or stand on their own in the Gallery section of a chapter, these photographs document the winning ways of two centuries of American women athletes. Look at them closely. Maybe you too will feel like you're taking a trip back in time.

ACKNOWLEDGMENTS

In July 1973, when I was a 19-year-old summer intern at my local newspaper, my editor assigned me to interview 1950s tennis great Althea Gibson. I prepared diligently, reading her autobiography, talking to people who had seen her play, digging up articles about her 1957 and 1958 Wimbledon and U.S. Nationals victories. Still, when I walked into her office, I was overwhelmed. Gibson was an imposing figure, too large somehow for a room cluttered with furniture and papers and books about business. I shook her hand, stammered hello, and sat down quickly, scanning my notes and trying to regain my composure. Just when I thought I was focused enough to ask a coherent question, I spotted Gibson's two Wimbledon plates. It suddenly hit me that I had come face-to-face with a legend.

It wasn't a great moment in the history of American women in sports, but it was a memorable one for me. Meeting a woman who had broken through racial barriers to become the top athlete in her sport made a powerful impression on a young journalist who still had trouble finding the confidence to conduct an interview. From that moment, a great respect for women athletes took root in me, along with a curiosity about what made them tick. I began clipping and saving articles about ground-breaking athletes and even wrote a college paper about early women tennis players. When it came time to write this book, all those years of unofficial research gave me a running start.

As I acknowledge those people who helped to make *Winning Ways* a reality, therefore, I have to start with Althea Gibson and Ed Scudder, the photographer who accompanied me to the Gibson interview and kept the conversation going while I struggled to get past my feelings of awe. I also would like to express my appreciation to the following people for their more recent support:

To all of the photo researchers at all of the agencies and archives, especially special consultant Grace How, Maja Keech of the Library of Congress Prints and Photographs Division, and Debbie Goodsite and Sarah Partridge of the Bettmann Archive.

To the librarians at the Englewood Public Library; Princeton University's Firestone Library; and the Johnson Public Library of Hackensack, N.J., for safeguarding the resources that were so crucial to my research.

To the women of the All-American Girls Professional Baseball League, especially Fran Janssen, Lou Arnold, and Gloria Elliott, for their continued encouragement and inspiration, and the late Shirley Stovroff, for her own

Althea Gibson puts a young writer at ease during our 1973 interview. At the time, she was the national director of the Pepsi-Cola Mobile Tennis Program, whose aim was to bring the game of paddle tennis to kids in inner-city communities. *Ed Scudder/The Herald-News*

ACKNOWLEDGMENTS

elegant analysis of the changing attitudes toward women in sports.

To Jill Safro, Felicia Halpert, and Liz Neporent, friends and colleagues who lent me books and articles and never were too busy to talk sports.

To Marc Aronson, for his confidence and guidance in helping this book take shape.

To my mother, my fitness role model, who has gone to exercise or aerobics every week since I was a toddler; my father, the best dad on the block, who taught me to hit line drives that broke windows; and my brother, still my number-one reference on sports and a very funny guy.

To Sheila Wolinsky, for her patience and her partnership, and for persevering as I watched Silver Bullets games with dinner and other women's sports events whenever I could find them on TV.

And to Hannah Sabrina Roth, age three, a runner, swimmer, and acrobat, for convincing me that the future of women's sports will be even brighter than the past.

F O R E W O R D
Raising the Banner

November 15, 1994, belonged to Martina Navratilova. That evening, New York's Madison Square Garden was packed with 17,131 fans, a record by far for a Tuesday night tennis match. The fans had come to watch the Virginia Slims Championships tournament, the final showdown for the top 16 women players of 1994. But more than that, they had come to honor Navratilova, who was competing in the final singles tournament of her 22-year career.

Navratilova's first-round opponent that Tuesday was Gabriela Sabatini, and the Argentinian refused to be awed by the historic importance of the occasion. As fans clutched their autographed Martina tennis balls, given free to every ticket holder, they watched Sabatini unleash a combination of stinging forehand passing shots and spinning backhand lobs that sent the 38-year-old Navratilova scrambling all over the court. There were moments of Martina greatness—a speeding forehand drive here, a perfectly placed half volley there. But Sabatini, who would go on to win the week-long tournament, was just too good.

After Sabatini closed out a 6–4, 6–2 victory, though, it was Navratilova who walked off the court to the louder applause. She made a quick trip to the locker room and then she was back, wearing a fresh T-shirt and smiling despite the loss. She stood in silence as the public-address announcer drew the crowd's attention to the overhead monitor, where a short film offered highlights of her career. The crowd saw a young, chubby Martina wearing a one-piece tennis dress with wide lapels. Then a more recognizable Martina, slimmer, somehow taller, sweeping up all the tennis balls her opponents hit at her and returning them with power and grace. Martina ran. Martina lunged. Martina lifted weights at a gym. And Martina shook hands with one opponent after another as she notched her 1,443 singles victories and 167 tournament singles titles.

When the film ended and the lights went on, the fans in the Garden stood as one and clapped. It was the end of an era, and they knew it. The player who had been deemed the finest woman athlete in tennis history, and, by some, the best woman athlete of all time, was calling it quits. But even as she retired, she was making history. In the final tribute of the evening, a banner proclaiming Navratilova's name was lifted to the rafters of the arena, joining those already there for outstanding players of New York's Knicks and Rangers. Navratilova's banner, to be displayed during all Madison Square Garden tennis tournaments, was the first at the Garden to honor a woman.

Martina Navratilova set a new standard for women's achievements in sports. She trained to win, ate to win, and played to win, and a whole generation of women athletes learned from her example. Yet Navratilova, and other female athletes of the 1980s and '90s, owed at least some of their success to the scores of women before them who defied attempts to keep them from exercising or playing sports. A century before Navratilova saw her name raised to the rafters, a male sportswriter warned that women who learned to smash and volley tennis balls the way men did might destroy the image of tennis as a refined game. In 1928, the Pope issued a letter condemning a public exhibition by female gymnasts, suggesting that the athletes "should think first of becoming good mothers of worthy sons." In 1967, Boston Marathon officials tried to rip the entry number off the chest of the first woman who dared to enter the men-only race.

The history of women's sports in the U.S. is the story of women who kept running, or vaulting, or volleying in spite of these critics. It is the story of individuals like Catharine Beecher, one of the first "exercise gurus" in the nation, who wrote a book on the benefits of physical fitness for women in 1856. And Ora Mae Washington, the 1930s national African American tennis champion who was not welcome to compete against white players and even today is left out of most histories of the game. And pitcher Jackie Mitchell, who struck out Babe Ruth and Lou Gehrig, only to see her accomplishment belittled by newspapers that claimed, "Her curves were too much for them!" It is the story of groups of women too, like the 1892 Smith College

Martina Navratilova takes in the moment as her banner is raised to the ceiling at Madison Square Garden. *Barton Silverman/NYT Pictures*

basketball players, the first women to embrace the sport. And the women's track teams of Tuskegee Institute, which dominated national and Olympic competitions from the late 1930s into the 1950s. It is the story of the clubs, colleges, teams, and leagues that gave women the chance to win— or lose—with their heads held high.

Winning Ways is a scrapbook filled with anecdotes and photographs, news reports and commentaries that capture some of the highlights and turning points in American women's sports. It is not an encyclopedia. It includes many, but certainly not all, of the athletes who helped make sports a bigger part of women's lives. Nor is it a straightforward chronicle of dates or events. Although the chapters unfold in chronological order, they present significant athletes in the social context of their times, weaving in ongoing themes such as changing clothing styles, the growth of the media, and evolving attitudes about femininity and competition. Ultimately, *Winning Ways* is a history of women in the United States told through the experiences of athletes whose love of sports led them to challenge assumptions about women's place in society. From the first croquet players after the Civil War to the America[3] sailing crew in 1995, the athletes in this book opened up new worlds for themselves and those who came after them. Like Martina Navratilova, they were driven by a determination to try their hardest, to do their best. When Madison Square Garden honors Navratilova by hanging her banner, it commemorates their efforts too.

THE 1800s
A Century of Progress

n 1892, when Frances Willard was 53 years old, she decided to learn how to ride a bicycle. Willard was president of the Women's Christian Temperance Union (WCTU), the largest women's organization of the nineteenth century. She approached this new challenge with the same care and determination that she used in planning the WCTU's campaigns to stop the sale of alcohol and win women the right to vote. Over a period of three months, Willard spent an average of 15 minutes a day on her bicycle, learning to balance, pedal, turn, dismount, and finally ride without help. She spent so much time with it that she even gave it a name, Gladys. "Gradually, item by item, I learned the location of every screw and spring, spoke and tire, and every beam and bearing that went to make up Gladys," she wrote in 1895. "It had to be learned before we could get on together."

Willard was one of more than a million American women who owned and rode bicycles in the 1890s. This bicycle craze was a turning point in American women's sports, the first time an athletic activity became widely popular among women from all walks of life. Cycling offered these women a sense of freedom they had not enjoyed since they were children. "I 'ran wild' until my sixteenth birthday, when the hampering long skirts were brought, with their accompanying corset and high heels," wrote Willard. "My work then changed from my beloved and breezy outdoor world to the indoor realm of study, teaching, writing, speaking." Like many women of the 1890s, Willard welcomed the chance for adventure and the feeling of power that came with riding a bicycle. She also believed that triumphing over the bicycle was symbolic of greater achievements. "I began to feel that myself plus the bicycle equaled myself plus the world," wrote Willard. "She who succeeds in gaining mastery of such an animal as Gladys, will gain the mastery of life."

Frances Willard was so inspired by her experience with the bicycle that she wrote a best-selling book urging other women to learn to ride. Its success shows how far attitudes toward American women in sports had come by the end of the nineteenth century. Before the Civil War, the athletic activities of Americans in the new nation were almost exclusively male. Men in cities gathered at their local taverns to play cards, bet on animal fights, and occasionally watch or take part in boxing matches. Male slaves spent their holidays playing ball, wrestling, dancing, boxing, and running footraces. Some also trained horses or rode in races at their masters' orders. Among the wealthiest classes, men were free to play baseball and cricket, and

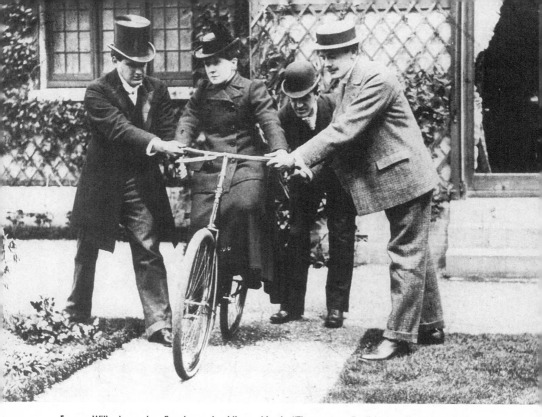

Frances Willard gets her first lesson in riding a bicycle. "Three young Englishmen, all strong-armed and accomplished bicyclers, held the machine while I climbed timidly into the saddle," wrote Willard. She named her bicycle Gladys because learning to ride brought her "gladness." *Courtesy of the Frances E. Willard Memorial Library*

to hunt, fish, and sail. Women, meanwhile, were largely limited to walking, dancing, and horseback riding.

Doctors and exercise specialists spent the greater part of the 1800s arguing about how much physical activity, if any, was healthy for women. Those who believed that women should refrain from exercise issued stories of the dreadful effects it could have. On October 26, 1827, *American Farmer* magazine warned that women who exercised too much were likely to grow small tumors on their ankle joints like those on the legs of young horses that were worked too hard. On February 11, 1860, *Harper's Weekly* contained "A Warning to Lady-Skaters," which reported that a young lady in Boston who tied her ice-skate laces too tightly cut off her circulation and had to have one foot amputated. Supporters of physical activity for women tried to meet such tactics with reason. In July 1892 the journal *Physical Education,* published by the Young Men's Christian Association (YMCA), focused on women. The editors argued that women needed physical strength and endurance because they were "the mothers of the race," and healthy mothers had healthy children. They also dismissed the belief that women were too weak to exercise. "The popular impression seems to be that as woman's muscles are weak therefore she should not be given work which demands that she shall have strength," wrote the editors. "The truth is exactly the reverse."

Clothing did much to hinder women's involvement in physical activity and sports. For most of the 1800s, middle- and upper-class women wore long dresses with as many as six or more skirts, called petticoats, underneath. They also conformed to the ideal of having an ample chest and a slim waist by wearing corsets. Corsets were undergarments, made of fabric and whalebone, that extended from the chest to the waist and were laced and tied tightly to push the chest up and out. Later in the century, this "tight lacing" would earn the scorn of many reformers, who accurately charged that it interfered with circulation, caused deformed ribs and weak muscles, and could even lead to death. The 1852 advice book *The Ladies' Indispensable Assistant* stated that "no woman who laces tight can have good shoulders, a straight spine, good lungs, sweet breath, or is fit to be a wife and mother." But corsets and petticoats

I owe my Graceful figure to Cooley's Cork Corset.

COOLEY'S CORK CORSET

Cooley's Cork Corset.

On the back of this advertising card, Cooley's promised that their corsets were "comfortable, easy, graceful, and healthful," because they used cork-covered steel instead of bone to shape a woman's figure. *Collection of the author* helped to give women an air of wealth and leisure, in sharp contrast to the simple, shapeless, functional clothing worn by farm women and factory workers. Before the Civil War, these undergarments were a status symbol, and upper-class women wore them even while engaging in sports.

Horseback riding was the first sport considered acceptable for American women, although reports from visitors to the United States indicate that some early horsewomen embraced it with a highly unfeminine spirit. During the 1790s, Frenchman Ferdinand Bayard wrote home about "skillful and fearless" female riders who raced against each other, and Venezuelan Francisco de Miranda noted that some women raced "with the best male riders for a wager." By the 1830s, though, *Godey's Lady's Book* and other magazines were advising horsewomen against joining fox hunts and racing contests. In 1830 *American Farmer* warned, "We do not, while thus admiring a lady on horseback, recommend that she should be able to keep up with the hounds in a stag or fox chase, nor run races for high bets." These magazines also insisted that women riders wear feminine clothing and urged them to ride side-saddle, sitting with the legs together on one side of the horse instead of separating them around the horse's back.

At the same time that women were arranging their corseted bodies on horseback, one pioneering teacher began to develop exercises specifically for them. Catharine Beecher was from a family of reformers. Her father and seven brothers were outspoken ministers, and her younger sister, Harriet Beecher Stowe, would go on to write the best-selling anti-slavery novel *Uncle Tom's Cabin*. Although

Catharine believed that a woman's rightful place was in the home, she also felt that young wives and mothers suffered because they lacked exercise and healthy diets. When she opened her first school for young women in 1823, and her second in 1837, she included calisthenics, or light gymnastic exercises, as part of the curriculum. Beecher set her calisthenics to music and described them as "grace without dancing." In 1856 she published *Physiology and Calisthenics*, possibly the first fitness manual for American women.

EXERCISE 88.

Word of Command—" Sidewise Movement!"

Fig. 49.

Place the body and limbs as in *Fig.* 49, leaning to the *left.* Then change the feet, and throw them into the same position, leaning to the *right.*

Count *one* at the first movement, and so on to *twelve.*

Catharine Beecher's 1856 manual, *Physiology and Calisthenics*, offered readers step-by-step instructions for many exercises. Casual clothes, such as those worn by the model, were considered acceptable as long as women exercised out of the sight of men. *Collection of the author*

Beecher set a precedent by linking education and exercise, and the founders of the women's colleges that were established after the Civil War followed her lead. When Matthew Vassar opened Vassar College in 1865, he included a special School of Physical Training with classes in riding, gardening, swimming, boating, skating, and "other physical accomplishments suitable for ladies to acquire . . . bodily strength and grace." Vassar housed its physical education activities in a "Calisthenium," which featured a gymnasium, bowling alleys, and a riding school. Ten years later, the newest women's college, Wellesley, offered its students a gymnasium for exercising and a lake for rowing and ice skating. After that, other women's schools and even some coed universities included athletic programs for their female students.

For the rest of the nineteenth century, American women's sports developed on two fronts, in colleges and in society at large. Colleges offered the perfect setting for exercise instructors to test their theories, so many schools had elaborate exercise programs. But students soon grew bored doing hour after hour of calisthenics, and their instructors began to teach them team sports. Toward the end of the century, college women were responsible for the surge of interest in basketball, volleyball, and the British game of field hockey.

Meanwhile, individual sports became popular among women outside of the colleges. The first new sport introduced after the Civil War, croquet, required participants to use a wooden mallet to knock a ball through a series of small arches set up around a lawn. Croquet was unique

This "fashion plate" from the April 1866 issue of *Godey's Lady's Book* shows stylishly dressed women enjoying a game of croquet. Monthly drawings such as this aimed to keep readers up-to-date on the latest fashions. The third woman from the right is described as wearing a "croquet dress of black alpaca, trimmed round the edge of the skirt, up the front, and up each breadth with bands of green silk cut into points." *Collection of Loretta and Joe Nolan*

because women and men took part in it together, but the competition was more social than serious, and there was no official croquet tournament for women. The first sport to offer women a chance for competition on a national level was archery. Twenty women entered the National Archery Championship in 1879, each shooting two rounds of 24 arrows standing 50 yards from the target, and 48 arrows standing 60 yards away.

While women perfected their skill in refined sports such as archery and croquet, interest in a decidedly unrefined sport began to sweep the nation. The sport was pedestrianism, or marathon walking, and the woman behind the craze was a British singer, actress, and musi-

Published in 1880, just one year after the first National Archery Championship for women, this cartoon, entitled "Bending Her Beau," offered pointed commentary on the abilities of female archers. *Library of Congress, LC-USZ62-17673*

cian named Madame Ada Anderson. In December 1878, Anderson arrived at Mozart Hall in Brooklyn, New York, to begin a month-long quest to walk 3,000 quarter miles in 3,000 quarter hours. With her husband and her trainers, she set up a track inside the building and put up a tent with a bed and a stove in the center of the track. On December 16, Anderson started her marathon. Every quarter hour, she would walk a quarter mile, which took five minutes or so, and then spend the balance of the 15 minutes resting, eating, or even singing for her audience. During the 3,000 quarter hours of her marathon, she never slept or rested more than 10 minutes at a time.

Few spectators made their way to Mozart Hall at the start of Madame Anderson's marathon, but as word spread, more and more people paid the daily charge of 24 cents to watch her walk. Among those who joined the crowd were a number of gamblers, who made the most of people's growing interest in the marathon by taking bets on whether Anderson would succeed. Anderson herself admitted that she was motivated by money. She told *The New York Times*, "I am willing, for a money consideration, to test this physical strength, this nervous force, and muscular power with which I've been gifted, to show that they will bear a certain strain. If I break down . . . if I fall helpless, or it may be, dead on the track, then I lose my money." In the end, Anderson's body withstood the test. She walked her last quarter mile, a month after she started, in a speedy 2 minutes, 38 seconds. Then she and her husband walked away with their share of the gate receipts, approximately $10,000.

Madame Anderson's walk ushered in a year of pedestrian contests for women. Women competed—against each other or, like Anderson, against the clock—to prove their endurance and strength. But the presence of gamblers and the fact that some athletes wore relatively skimpy costumes, sometimes even showing their bare knees, gave pedestrianism an unsavory reputation. When contest promoters began to cut corners, pushing the women to walk longer and not offering adequate food and medical care, the bad publicity caused the sport to lose its appeal. By 1880, pedestrian contests for women had all but disappeared. Although their popularity was short-lived, these events are noteworthy for two important reasons. First, pedestrianism was one of the earliest sports in American history to put women's endurance to the test. Second, these contests marked the first time, but certainly not the last, that promoters used the sex appeal of women athletes to sell a sport to the public.

At about the same time Madame Anderson was preparing to bring pedestrianism to the United States, another woman, Mary Outerbridge, introduced a new sport to the country-club set. Outerbridge had played the game of lawn tennis on vacation in Bermuda in 1874, and she returned home with rackets, a net, tennis balls, and a brush to mark the lines of the court. She convinced her brother to set up a court at the Staten Island Cricket and Baseball Club in New York, and soon the male club members were playing tennis instead of cricket. By the 1880s women were enjoying tennis matches at country clubs too, and in 1887 the first women's

Corsets, petticoats, and long skirts were part of the uniform for early women tennis players. This 1886 portrait of male and female tennis champions at Newport, Rhode Island, shows that men dressed for the game in slightly more comfortable attire. *Library of Congress, LC-USZ62-33741*

national tennis tournament was held. Even after that, writers complained that women tennis players needed to adapt their clothing to truly play competitively. "It is much wiser to play without corsets," suggested one author, "although it must be admitted that few women do."

With so many new sports available to women in the 1880s and '90s, attitudes toward women's clothing finally did begin to change. Reform took the greatest leap forward after the invention of the light-framed bicycle, called the safety, in 1888. Before the safety, bicycles had a huge wheel in the front and a tiny one in the back and were quite difficult to ride. The safety had two wheels of similar size driven by a chain, which made riding much easier. (Frances Willard's Gladys was a safety.) In the 1890s women embraced cycling and the safety in great numbers, and most of them refused to ride in corsets and long skirts. Instead, some wore bloomers, calf-length pants with puffy legs that had been introduced 40 years before by women's rights advocate Amelia Bloomer. Others went a less radical route and wore simple skirts and blouses, shortening the skirts several inches so that the material didn't get caught in the bicycle wheels.

Bloomers were a passing fad, but the bicycle had a lasting effect on women's clothing as well as on their participation in sports. "To men, rich and poor, the bicycle is an unmixed blessing, but to women it is deliverance, revolution, salvation," wrote sportswoman Anna de Koven in the August 1895 issue of *Cosmopolitan* magazine. "It is impossible to overestimate the potentialities of this exercise in the curing of . . . ills of womankind, both physical and mental, or to calculate the far-reaching effects of its influence in the matters of dress and social reform." Pioneer feminist Susan B. Anthony agreed, stating simply that the bicycle did "more to emancipate woman than anything else in the world."

As women everywhere rode to their own personal freedom on their bicycles, college women got their first large-scale lessons in teamwork by playing the last important new sport of the nineteenth century, basketball. Invented in 1891 by YMCA instructor James Naismith, basketball quickly caught the attention of Senda Berenson, a 23-year-old gymnastics teacher at Smith College in Northampton, Massachusetts. Berenson read an article about basketball by Naismith, and she was impressed that the game "combined both the physical development of gymnastics and the abandon and delight of true play." Still, Berenson was concerned that she might offend parents and college officials if she had her female students play a "men's" game. So she adapted Naismith's rules and developed a fast-paced, but less strenuous, "women's" game. Berenson divided the court into three equal sections and required players to stay in their assigned section. She also outlawed stealing and ruled that players could hold the ball for only three seconds and dribble the ball three times in a row.

Berenson's changes served to reassure those concerned that basketball was a suitable game for women, and word soon spread to other colleges. While the first schools to embrace basketball were in the East, colleges on the West Coast quickly followed suit. As it happened, the first women's basketball game between colleges involved two

While women's basketball was first played at the college level, the game soon spread to high schools. In this 1899 photograph, girls at Western High School in Washington, D.C., strain for the ball as their teacher (in the white shirt) looks on. *Library of Congress, LC-USZ62-71237*

western schools. On April 4, 1896, teams from Stanford University and the University of California at Berkeley met at Armory Hall in San Francisco. The Berkeley team refused to play if men were admitted, so the contest took place in front of 500 female fans. "The fighting was hard and the playing was good," reported the *San Francisco Examiner*. "The girls jumped, scrambled, and fell over one another on the floor, but they didn't mind it. They were up quick as a flash, chasing after the ball again." In the end, the contest was close, although low scoring. With one point awarded for each basket, Stanford came out on top, 2–1.

29

As the nineteenth century drew to a close, American women were freer than ever before to dress comfortably, exercise, and take part in sports. Instead of picturing the ideal American woman seated primly in her corseted gown, magazines and advertisements increasingly pictured her enjoying physical activity. Even science was on the woman athlete's side. A study at Wellesley College in 1893 showed that students who practiced gymnastics or rowing over a five-month period were stronger and had greater lung capacities than students who had no regular exercise. But while women athletes had come far in the 1800s, they still had a long way to go. Women were deliberately left out of the first modern Olympic Games, held in Athens, Greece, in 1896. And many of the athletic opportunities that women enjoyed at the turn of the century were open only to well-to-do whites, not to minorities or the poor. As the new century dawned, these women would begin to demand a chance to even the score.

By the time this poster was printed in 1896, women were buying 25 to 30 percent of all new bicycles. Manufacturers portrayed women riders as healthy and happy, although this Stormer rider has not adopted the more comfortable attire worn by many of her sisters. *Library of Congress, LC-USZ62-24633*

This 1930 timeline shows the general dates when various sports were added to the physical education programs of 12 women's colleges in the United States. The colleges are listed in the boxes at the bottom. *From* The History of Physical Education in Colleges for Women, *by Dorothy S. Ainsworth, A. S. Barnes and Company, 1930*

1 9 0 0 – 1 9 1 9
Pathfinders

On October 24, 1901, Annie Edson Taylor celebrated her forty-third birthday with a big splash. As thousands cheered her on, the Michigan schoolteacher stepped into an oak barrel about 4½ feet high and 3 feet across. She slipped her arms through a pair of leather shoulder straps, placed a pillow over her head, and ordered that the barrel be bolted shut. Moments later, at 4:05 P.M., Taylor and the barrel were set adrift in the waters leading to Niagara Falls. They floated toward the roaring waterfall, picking up speed as the current grew more and more powerful. Finally, at 4:23, they reached the edge of the Falls and disappeared, plunging 173 feet into the heavy mist below. "I was whirled about like a top, and the water seemed to come in on me in bucketfuls," Taylor recalled after she and the barrel were successfully pulled to shore. "I held tightly to the handles and thought only of preventing my head from striking the top of the barrel. Once, for a moment, I seemed to lose my senses. I struck rocks three times."

Annie Edson Taylor was the first person, man or woman, to go over Niagara Falls in a barrel and live to tell about it. What possessed her to risk life and limb to "shoot the Falls"? Before the plunge, Taylor said she was giving it a try simply because "Nobody has ever done that," but afterward she confided that she also had another motive. Taylor owed a lot of money on a cattle ranch that she had bought in Texas, and she hoped to earn enough from her newfound fame to get out of debt. Following her historic moment, though, Taylor declared that she wouldn't do it

Moments after her daring plunge, Annie Edson Taylor gingerly makes her way to dry land. Based on interviews with Taylor's descendants, Canadian author Dwight Whalen disputes accounts reporting her age at the time of the plunge. He thinks she was 63, not 43. *Special Collections Department, Niagara Falls (N.Y.) Public Library*

Taylor never became rich and famous, even after her celebrated feat. Shortly before she died on April 29, 1921, she observed, "I did what no other woman in the world had nerve enough to do, only to die a pauper." *Special Collections Department, Niagara Falls (N.Y.) Public Library*

again, even for a million dollars. "If it was with my dying breath I would caution anyone against attempting the feat," she said. "I would sooner walk up to the mouth of a cannon, knowing it was going to blow me to pieces, than to make another trip over the Falls."

Taylor's honest reaction to the danger she had faced did not dissuade other women from undertaking equally challenging athletic exploits. The early years of the twentieth century saw the emergence of a new breed of American sportswoman, the daredevil. Whether they climbed mountains, raced automobiles, flew airplanes, or shot the Falls, these women seemed determined to show that they could do anything men could do, and some things men could not. Their daring and sense of adventure were held up as examples for other women. After Dora Keen scaled Alaska's Mt. Blackburn, 16,400 feet above sea level, Anna de Koven wrote in *Good Housekeeping,* "Few of the friends whom Miss Keen left behind in their comfortable homes have any realization of the hardships endured, even glorified, by this fearless young woman." Keen started out with seven male Alaskan mountain climbers and nine dogs, reported de Koven, but the storms, avalanches, and below-zero temperatures took their toll. "So severe were the climatic conditions that the men deserted singly and in pairs until only two men and none of the dogs remained with Miss Keen to finish the trip."

Female daredevils came from all classes of society, though most of them were white and many were unmarried. Their motivations for taking risks varied as greatly as their backgrounds, but their actions were dramatic proof that the women of the twentieth century had little in common with the frail, overprotected ladies of the past. Daredevils embodied the qualities of what women's rights advocates and the press called the New Woman. The New Woman dressed more comfortably than her foremothers, thanks in part to the revolution in clothing brought about by the bicycle. She was more likely than her foremothers to have interests outside the home, working or, if she was

The New Woman was a symbol of strength and independence, but the press wasn't above making fun of her. In this 1901 picture, the photographer has reversed the male and female roles to an exaggerated degree. *Library of Congress, LC-USZ62-98406*

wealthy, joining women's clubs or reform groups. She also was more likely to be educated. By 1900, 80 percent of the colleges, universities, and professional schools in the United States accepted women. From 1900 to 1920, the number of female students at these women's and coed schools grew from 85,000 to 283,000.

Women in the early twentieth century also were in the

37

public eye more than women before them. In the early 1800s it was considered a disgrace for a woman's name to appear in a newspaper or magazine, but a hundred years later, women's achievements were regularly celebrated in print. One of the new century's first celebrity daredevils was a magazine writer who recorded the details of her exploits herself. Harriet Quimby was a 27-year-old reporter and drama critic for *Leslie's Illustrated Weekly* when she learned to fly an airplane in 1911. On August 1, 1911, she became the first American woman to earn a pilot's license, and eight months later, on April 16, 1912, she became the first woman ever to fly across the English Channel.

Harriet Quimby, dressed for the cold in an open airplane, readies for one of her first flights in 1911. Quimby firmly believed that women had a future in flying. "There is no sport that affords the same amount of excitement and enjoyment, and exacts in return so little muscular strength," she wrote in 1912. "It is easier than walking, driving, automobiling; easier than golf or tennis. I should say it is the ideal pastime for the lazy sportsman." *Library of Congress, LC-USZ62-15070*

Quimby flew in the early days of aviation, less than 10 years after Orville and Wilbur Wright invented the airplane. In 1912, planes had open cockpits, with no protection from rain or wind and no seat belts or parachutes for emergencies. Plane crashes were all too common, especially during landings, and a number of pilots lost their lives. Quimby scoffed at any talk of hazards. In an article for *Good Housekeeping* she wrote, "The men flyers have given out the impression that aeroplaning is very perilous work, something that an ordinary mortal should not dream of attempting; but when I saw how easily the men flyers manipulated their machines I said I could fly. While I have not exactly followed in their footsteps, I have at least accomplished something along the line of flying." By the time these words were printed, though, Quimby's name had been added to the casualty list. On July 1, 1912, at the end of a 20-mile flight around Boston Harbor, her plane hit an air pocket, throwing a passenger and then Quimby into the shallow bay below. The *Boston Post* noted her death with words appropriate for a true New Woman. "Harriet Quimby, ambitious to be among the pathfinders, asked no handicap on account of her sex," the *Post* said. "She took her chances like a man and died like one."

At the same time that female daredevils were challenging people's assumptions of what women could do, more traditional sports were becoming an accepted part of girls' educations and women's lives. Colleges increasingly emphasized team and individual sports over calisthenics and gymnastics, and educators justified this change by pointing out that sports helped girls develop character as well as physical fitness. They listed courage, concentration, self-control, and fair play as some of the qualities female students gained through sports. In 1903 a description of field day at Vassar reassured readers that team loyalty quickly overshadowed the more selfish goal of personal glory. During this day of track-and-field events between classes, first-year students got a chance to set a school record and earn a pink V. The freshman "takes the hurdles one by one," reported Alice Katharine Fallows in *The Century Illustrated Monthly Magazine.* "With brain on fire, throat of parchment, feet of lead, she makes a last spurt into the arms of her friends beyond the tape, and breaks the record. The freshmen let loose pandemonium. The class cheer bursts forth, and the winner's name rings out at the end. But in the moment of her triumph, with the excitement and enthusiasm surging about her, her first exultant thought is not, 'I've won my V,' but, 'I've helped my class.' "

As college sports for women became widespread, educators grew concerned that there were no official rules to regulate them. Basketball players at Bryn Mawr, for instance, ran all over the court and were allowed to steal the ball. Those at Smith followed Senda Berenson's revised rules and could not "snatch or bat the ball." In an attempt to standardize play, physical educators began to form organizations specifically dedicated to women's sports. In 1899 the first of these groups, the Women's Basketball Rules Committee, officially adopted Smith College's rules as the standard for women's basketball. The idea of drafting separate rules for women's and men's college sports slowly took

As fans cheer them on, students at Vassar College enjoy a game of outdoor basketball in May 1913. *Library of Congress, LC-USZ62-22263*

hold, and in 1917 the American Physical Education Association (APEA) formed the Committee on Women's Athletics (CWA) to do just that. The CWA soon developed rules for women's field hockey, swimming, track and field, and soccer.

Underlying the adoption of these separate rules was the widely accepted belief that women were weaker than men and did not have the endurance to play rigorous sports. This notion harkened back to the early nineteenth century, when doctors warned that too much exercise could cause a woman physical harm and permanently damage her ability to have children. By the end of the century, most doctors accepted the evidence that exercise actually made women more fit for childbirth. Still, they remained concerned about the effects of sports on women's nerves and on their bodies during menstruation. In the 1918–1919 *Official Basket Ball Guide for Women,* Dr. J. Anna Norris recommended strict rules to keep girls from playing basketball during the first three days of their menstrual periods. Similar measures were endorsed by other doctors as late as 1959.

If adopting separate rules was designed to protect women athletes, it also aimed to make sure women remained weaker and less aggressive than men. In the early twentieth century, there was a growing fear that women who took part in sports would lose the qualities that made them uniquely female. Dr. Dudley A. Sargent addressed this in "Are Athletics Making Girls Masculine? A Practical Answer to a Question Every Girl Asks" in the March 1912 issue of the *Ladies Home Journal.* A leader in physical education since the 1870s, Sargent admitted that many sports did cause women to develop traits that were traditionally thought of as male. "Physically all forms of athletic sports and most physical exercises tend to make women's figures more masculine," he wrote, "inasmuch as they tend to broaden the shoulders, deepen the chest, narrow the hips, and develop the muscles of the arms, back and legs." But Sargent believed in exercise too much to declare sports bad for women. Instead, he called for moderation. "Women as a class cannot stand a prolonged mental or physical strain as well as men," wrote Sargent.

He recommended that women's games adopt shorter playing times, longer rest periods, and lighter equipment that could be adjusted according to each woman's needs.

Beyond the effects of sports on a woman's body, Sargent and other physical educators were concerned about the effects on her emotions. Sargent added his voice to the growing chorus that warned against competition for girls, denouncing schools and colleges that fed rivalries with talk of school pride. "Under the sway of these powerful impulses," he wrote, "the individual is not only forced to do her best, but to do better than her best, though she breaks down in her efforts to surpass her previous records." Instead of glorifying competition, Sargent endorsed events such as Vassar's field day, designed to encourage athletes to work together for the good of their teams. Senda Berenson's basketball rules too were written with teamwork in mind. Players had no choice but to rely on each other when they were barred from leaving their third of the court. By stressing teamwork over individual glory, these educators thought they had found a way to ensure that women maintained their nurturing, cooperative natures while taking part in sports. But limiting the enthusiasm of women athletes was not as easy as they wanted to believe. The issue of controlling competition in women's sports would be debated again and again throughout the twentieth century.

For African American women athletes at the beginning of the century, controlling competition was less of an issue than finding opportunities to compete. Two factors combined to greatly limit the athletic outlets for black women and to delay the rise of the African American female

This team portrait, taken sometime between 1900 and 1920, shows the student basketball players at the National Training School for Women and Girls in Washington, D.C. *Library of Congress, LC-USZ62-113555*

sports star until the 1920s and '30s. First, few African Americans were accepted into the mainstream women's and coed colleges where basketball, field hockey, and other women's sports developed. Second, women students who attended private black colleges at the turn of the century found that those schools virtually ignored sports for women. Black women and girls, therefore, were forced to develop their athletic abilities outside of school. The "colored" branches of the YMCA and YWCA that opened in some cities starting in 1893 offered women such activities as gymnastics, fencing, basketball, and tennis. The sports clubs for schoolchildren in many northern cities gave girls a chance to be coached in team sports such as basketball and to compete in individual events, including baseball throws, running races, and swimming.

One female African American athlete did rise to fame before the 1920s, in the unlikely sport of tennis. Tennis was not a pastime offered by most Y's or sports clubs, and blacks were not admitted to the private white country clubs where the game was played. The United States Lawn Tennis Association, which ran the U.S. national tournament, had an unwritten rule barring blacks. Despite these obstacles, African American college students learned the game and started to put together tournaments. Like the baseball players in the Negro leagues, these tennis players created their own environment in which to compete. In 1916, they formed the American Tennis Association (ATA), a group dedicated to promoting tennis among black men, women, boys, and girls. When the ATA held its first national tournament in August 1917, Lucy Diggs Slowe won the women's singles crown, becoming the first African American national female champion in any sport. She took the national title again in 1921. Slowe went on to become the principal of the first junior high school in Washington, D.C., and the Dean of Women at Howard University. She was celebrated as a role model in the African American community.

During the years from 1900 to 1919, sports became an accepted part of girls' and women's lives. Individual efforts by daredevils such as Annie Edson Taylor and Harriet Quimby brought Americans face-to-face with a new breed of women who were as brave as they were bold. Team sports played at colleges, Y's, and neighborhood clubs gave female athletes a chance to learn teamwork and fans a chance to admire their skills. All the

45

while, men and women tried to get comfortable with this role of woman as athlete. In the world at large, women began to take on other new roles. In 1917 and 1918, when American men left their jobs to fight in World War I, their sisters, mothers, wives, and daughters filled in for them. They drove ambulances, built weapons, worked in oil refineries, and enlisted as clerical aides in the Navy and Marines. Soon after the war ended, women in the United States won a final victory. On August 26, 1920, Tennessee became the thirty-sixth state to ratify the Nineteenth Amendment to the U.S. Constitution, giving women the right to vote in all elections. As Americans entered the 1920s, it was clear that the New Woman, educated, political, powerful, and athletic, was here to stay.

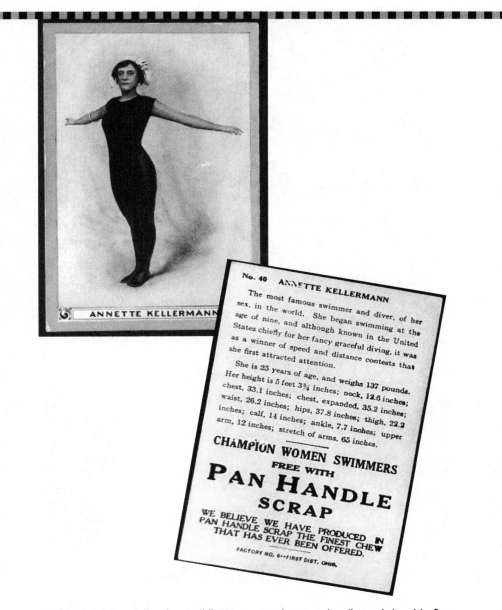

No. 40 ANNETTE KELLERMANN

The most famous swimmer and diver, of her sex, in the world. She began swimming at the age of nine, and although known in the United States chiefly for her fancy graceful diving, it was as a winner of speed and distance contests that she first attracted attention.

She is 25 years of age, and weighs 137 pounds. Her height is 5 feet 3¾ inches; neck, 12.6 inches; chest, 33.1 inches; chest, expanded, 35.2 inches; waist, 26.2 inches; hips, 37.8 inches; thigh, 22.2 inches; calf, 14 inches; ankle, 7.7 inches; upper arm, 12 inches; stretch of arms, 65 inches.

CHAMPION WOMEN SWIMMERS
FREE WITH
PAN HANDLE
SCRAP

WE BELIEVE WE HAVE PRODUCED IN PAN HANDLE SCRAP THE FINEST CHEW THAT HAS EVER BEEN OFFERED.

FACTORY NO. 6—FIRST DIST. OHIO.

ANNETTE KELLERMANN

Champion swimmer and diver Annette Kellermann appeared on several trading cards issued by Pan Handle Scrap, a brand of chewing tobacco. A native of Australia, Kellermann gained notoriety in 1907 when she ventured onto Revere Beach in Boston wearing a one-piece bathing suit. She was one of the first women to wear such a suit in public. *Collection of the author*

An unnamed woman proudly takes aim with her trap-shooting rifle in April 1914. *Library of Congress, Lot 11146-8*

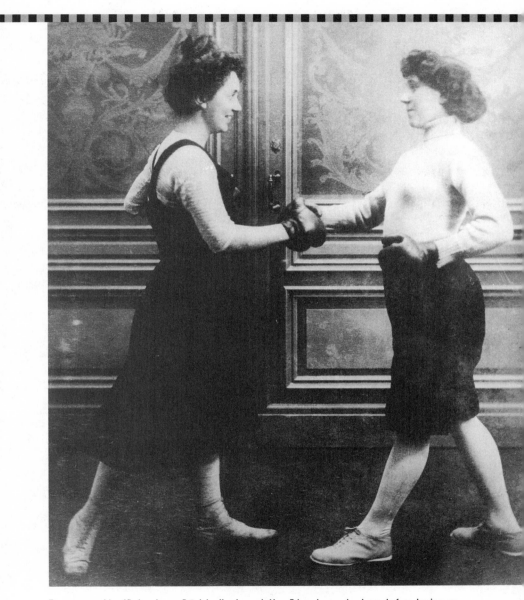

Two women, identified only as Fräulein Kussin and Mrs. Edwards, touch gloves before boxing on March 7, 1912. Women were not encouraged to box or even attend boxing matches at the time. In 1901 a Baltimore woman was arrested for watching a prize fight. Twenty-one years later, the mayor of Cleveland, Ohio, ruled that any boxing club that let women buy tickets to its matches would have its license revoked. *Library of Congress, Lot 11146-18*

THE TENNIS GIRL
She likes to court in the court,
Thinks tennis "the jolliest sport!"
And shouts "thirty all!"
As she whacks at the ball
With many a cowlike cavort!

This 1905 postcard takes a sarcastic swipe at female tennis players. The upside-down writing at the top is part of the sender's message, "Suppose you will not play much these cold days." *Collection of the author*

1 9 2 0 – 1 9 2 9
The Golden Age of Sports

On August 6, 1926, editorial writers at *The Daily News* of London, England, decided to offer their opinion on the issue of women in sports. Their editorial, published in the next day's paper, stated what they thought was obvious: "Even the most uncompromising champion of the rights and capacities of women must admit that in contests of physical skill, speed and endurance they must remain forever the weaker sex." The newspaper's timing couldn't have been worse. As the editorial was being written, reporters less than 100 miles away were covering what W. O. McGeehan of *The New York Herald-Tribune* called "the greatest sports story in the world," and that story involved a woman. At 9:40 P.M. on August 6, Gertrude Ederle waded onto the beach at Kingsdown, England, after a 14-hour, 31-minute swim from Cape Gris-Nez, France. The 19-year-old American had battled brutal waves, stinging jellyfish, chilling water, and blinding fog to become the first woman to successfully swim across

the English Channel. She'd made the trip almost two hours faster than any of the five men who had swum the Channel before her.

Ederle's feat was big news across the United States and around the world. American writers and politicians praised the three-time Olympic medalist as a hero. "Gertrude Ederle has all the qualities that go to make up the kind of heroine whom America will ungrudgingly and freely worship and honor for her splendid accomplishment," *The New York Times* declared on August 7. "The record of her 19 years shows her to be courageous, determined, modest, sportsmanlike, generous, unaffected and perfectly poised." When Ederle returned to the United States, a record crowd of two million people came out to honor her at a ticker-tape parade down New York City's Broadway. President Calvin Coolidge called her "America's best girl." The William Morris talent agency signed her to a $2,000-a-week contract to tour the country, demonstrating her swimming style and answering questions about the Channel swim.

America's overwhelming reception for Ederle indicated the new level of enthusiasm with which athletes were received during the 1920s. In the years following World War I, the last remnants of the prim-and-proper nineteenth century gave way as the nation's character and

Gertrude Ederle is covered with grease to keep her warm as she shakes hands with a well-wisher before starting her swim from France to England. Despite Ederle's record-breaking feat, British officials didn't welcome her with open arms. Before they let her enter the country, they made her wait for hours and then quizzed her about herself and her family. Why? It seems that in all the excitement, no one had remembered to bring along Ederle's passport! *Library of Congress Prints and Photographs Division*

During the 1920s, some young women shocked their elders by wearing outfits such as this one, described as "a fetching little tailormade ensemble of mannish material." The short skirt and the model's short hair and cloche hat were other trademarks of '20s fashion. *AP/Wide World Photos*

culture underwent a radical change. Suddenly Americans, especially young Americans, seemed to crave excitement. Young people rebelled by wearing daring clothes, listening to jazz, doing fast and furious dances that their parents found scandalous, and generally looking at life with a hard-edged sense of humor. Young women cut their hair short, raised the hemlines of their skirts, smoked cigarettes, wore makeup, and flirted with young men. This was the Jazz Age, the Roaring Twenties, with silent movies, radio programs, automobiles, and newspapers and magazines linking the country from coast to coast as never before. Even the concept of what was news changed. In 1919, the nation's first half-size "tabloid" newspaper, *The New York Daily News*, began publishing. By 1924 it had the highest circulation of any paper in the United States. *The Daily News* and other tabloids focused on stories involving sex or violence that lent themselves to screaming headlines and provocative photographs. The "news" no longer had to be important; it just had to be exciting.

Sports played a big part in this energetic decade. People headed to beaches and ball fields in record numbers, and for women, the voluptuous look of the nineteenth century was replaced by a new, thinner ideal. Besides playing sports and looking athletic, people became passionate sports fans, following the exploits of their favorite stars in person, on the radio, and in the newspapers. The decade of the 1920s, often called the Golden Age of Sports, also was the Golden Age of Sports Reporting. Full-time sportswriters recounted athletic events with dramatic and colorful language that made readers feel as if they were part of the action. This helped to make sports into a form of entertainment every bit as popular as the movies. Newspapers expanded their sports pages until they grew into sports sections. In 1890, the two daily newspapers in the small city of Muncie, Indiana, devoted an average of just under four pages per day to sports. By 1923, that average had increased to 13 pages per day. Major sports events became front-page news. Gertrude Ederle's swim was reported as it happened over the radio in 1926. The next day it was the lead story on page one of *The New York Times,* with detailed accounts of the feat from reporters who had followed Ederle in a tugboat for all 14-plus hours. It's no wonder that Americans came out in force to welcome "Our Trudy" home.

With all of the hype, fans sometimes became more interested in the athletes than in the sports that they played. Such was the case with French tennis player Suzanne Lenglen and her rival, Californian Helen Wills. In the 1920s, when Lenglen and Wills dominated the game, tennis was still an elite sport enjoyed mostly by middle- and upper-class men and women at colleges and country clubs. Yet at times, there was enough interest in these two female stars to warrant articles about one or both of them almost every day. Thanks to their different backgrounds and personalities, sportswriters helped to make Lenglen and Wills symbols that fans could root for or against. People had opinions on which woman was better, even if they had never seen either of them play.

Both women made important contributions to the

Ten years after she swam her way into the record books, Gertrude Ederle looks over her scrapbook with one of her sisters. Only 29 at the time of this photograph, Ederle was plagued by a hearing impairment and constant back pains, results of her English Channel swim. *Library of Congress Prints and Photographs Division*

game. When Lenglen played her first Wimbledon tournament in 1919, she showed up in a one-piece, calf-length, short-sleeved cotton dress that became the new standard for women tennis players. She also wore a "bandeau," or headband, woven from two yards of silk cloth. Lenglen's daring style of dress was equaled only by her daring style of play. With blazing strokes, excellent control, and lightning speed, she swept through her first Wimbledon, taking the title from the defending champion, Dorothy

Lambert Chambers. She would win five more Wimbledon singles titles in the next seven years. Helen Wills did her own part to simplify women's tennis clothes, most often playing in a sleeveless, white, knee-length dress, and a white visor to keep the sun out of her eyes. She entered her first U.S. National tennis championships as a 15-year-old, and her pigtails and easygoing manner made her a crowd favorite. So did her performance on the court. Wills had a powerful serve and a strong baseline game, rarely missing with her groundstrokes and rarely changing her intense, determined expression. She would go on to be one of the most dominant American women in tennis history, winning eight Wimbledon singles crowns and seven U.S. National women's singles titles.

Wills and Lenglen played each other in singles only once, on February 16, 1926, at a small tennis club in Cannes, France. The match pitted "Sizzling Suzanne," as sportswriter Grantland Rice called Lenglen, against the mild-mannered "American Girl," and the reporters couldn't get enough. "No tennis match deserved the attention this one received," Helen Wills wrote seven years later in *The Saturday Evening Post.* "Our match was pounced upon by the newspaper correspondents, who waited on the courts or else in the bar at the corner. I know that I, and probably Mademoiselle Lenglen, too, was inclined to think that the outcome of the match meant more than it really did. It is not always easy to maintain a sense of proportion at a time like this." Wills was clearly

Looking more like they're about to attend a ball than to hit one, Suzanne Lenglen, *left,* and Helen Wills arrive on the tennis court for their 1926 match. *UPI/Bettmann*

the challenger, the younger woman who had come to meet the champion on her home ground. Throughout the match, Lenglen managed to keep her off balance. She ran Wills all over with her crosscourt drives and mixed in some drop shots to change the pace. Despite a rally in the second set, Wills lost to the woman she would later call "the greatest player I have met upon the court." The final score was 6–3, 8–6.

Lenglen turned professional soon after her meeting with Wills, choosing to be paid to play exhibition matches instead of entering tournaments such as Wimbledon and the U.S. Nationals, which then were open only to amateurs. With Lenglen out of the picture, Helen Wills ruled the tennis world. Meanwhile, in the parallel universe of African American sports, a champion emerged who might have given Wills a run for her money. Ora Mae Washington of Philadelphia, Pennsylvania, held her tennis racket halfway up the handle when she played, but her unusual style and her lightning speed got results. She won the American Tennis Association singles crown every year from 1929 through 1935 and then again in 1937. She also won the women's doubles title every year from 1928 through 1936. During the heart of Washington's winning streak, the *Chicago Defender*, an African American newspaper, reported that "Her superiority is so evident that her competitors are frequently beaten before the first ball

Ora Mae Washington poses with her tennis racket. When she wasn't playing tennis, Washington was the captain and top scorer of the *Philadelphia Tribune* girls' basketball team, which traveled around the nation challenging African American and white squads. *International Tennis Hall of Fame and Tennis Museum at the Newport Casino, Newport, Rhode Island*

crosses the net." Since ATA matches were rarely reported in the mainstream press, however, Washington was unknown outside of black America. When Helen Wills refused Washington's request for a match, not many people realized that she was saying no to one of the few players who might have beaten her.

While the 1920s saw the spotlight fall on a number of outstanding female athletes, not everyone was pleased with the sudden popularity of women's competitive sports. Starting in 1923, the nation's female physical educators launched a campaign to take control of women's sports and limit competition for women. They did so

The media frenzy that accompanied the Lenglen–Wills match is evident from the mass of photographers that awaited them. *UPI/Bettmann*

through the Women's Division of the National Amateur Athletic Federation (NAAF), an organization formed to promote a higher level of physical fitness for all Americans. Led by Lou Henry Hoover, wife of future President Herbert Hoover, the Women's Division aimed to protect women athletes from people who hoped to exploit their sex appeal or money-making potential. Hoover and her followers felt that women should not compete in the Olympic Games or on interscholastic high-school or college teams, and they denounced sports programs sponsored by businesses for their female employees. They especially targeted women's athletic programs run by men. "Physical education has too long been in the hands of school men and professional coaches," wrote educator Agnes Wayman in 1924. "When we see our adolescent high school girls playing long schedules of outside games, traveling around the country . . . wearing immodest clothing before mixed audiences . . . we know that it's time something sane and intelligent was done."

Efforts by the Women's Division to rein in women's sports were in direct opposition to those of another organization, the Amateur Athletic Union (AAU). Founded in 1888 by a group of sports clubs, the AAU sponsored a national women's swimming meet in 1916, and later added women's competitions in track and field (1924), basketball (1926), and gymnastics (1931). But the Women's Division and its backers charged that the AAU was more concerned with the money it made from entry fees and gate receipts than with the welfare of its athletes. In July 1929, sportswriter John Tunis endorsed the Women's Division's

During the 1920s, advertisements for everything from wristwatches to automobiles used images of athletic women to get people's attention. This 1928 ad for Bromo Quinine cold tablets and this 1929 ad for Kellogg's Pep Bran Flakes cereal both communicated the healthy effects of their products by showing women playing sports. *Bromo Quinine, collection of the author; Kellogg's Pep Bran Flakes, reprinted with permission ®, © 1929 Kellogg Company*

point of view with an article titled "Women and the Sport Business" in *Harper's Monthly Magazine*. "On the one hand is an active and articulate group [including the AAU] . . . attempting to drag women's sport into the morass of hypocrisy into which masculine sport has sunk," wrote Tunis. "On the other hand is a group . . . of idealists [the Women's Division] who are anxious to keep the American girl from this commercialized competition, to safeguard her health by placing her athletic activities under the direction of properly qualified women supervisors, and to provide for her a program of games which will spread a love of sport not only among the minority but also among the majority of the women of the United States."

With the motto "A team for everyone and everyone on a team," the Women's Division wanted females to have fun playing sports whether or not they were good athletes. Their "platform for sporting ideals" held that women should compete for their own enjoyment rather than for the enjoyment of fans. It stressed that coaches should not push female athletes too hard or sacrifice an athlete's health for the sake of the sport. It sought to downplay the successes of the strongest athletes by offering only awards or prizes with little monetary value. And it discouraged publicity that focused on individuals instead of team or group efforts.

Although the Women's Division was not able to impose its wishes on all aspects of women's sports, it did succeed in taking control of the programs in high schools and colleges. When the Women's Division was formed in 1923, 22 percent of U.S. colleges had varsity sports teams for women. By 1930, that rate had dropped to 12 percent. From the 1930s through the 1950s, most schools did not offer women's interscholastic programs. While female students at these schools continued to learn the basics of sports, they hardly ever got the chance to test their skills in highly competitive situations, as their brothers did. This policy against competition for girls might have saved some athletes from exploitation, but it also helped to cement the differences between boys and girls and the roles they were expected to play in American life. Boys retained their place as leaders and tough, competitive risk-takers, while girls were taught to be modest, supportive, and restrained. In this atmosphere, any girl who pursued sports outside of school ran the risk of seeming odd, or more masculine than she was supposed to be.

Concerns that women were not tough enough for competitive sports were fueled by an episode at the 1928 Olympic Games. The incident involved track and field, a sport that Women's Division members objected to because it focused on a few super-fast athletes and its uniforms were skimpy and revealing. Most Olympic officials disapproved of women's track-and-field events too, but after a series of successful international women's track meets, they added five events to the program on a trial basis. The problem came in the 800-meter run, a distance of about half a mile. It turned out that a number of the women who entered the 800 did not have proper training. As John Tunis described it, "Below us on the cinder path were eleven wretched women, five of whom dropped out before the finish, while five collapsed after reaching the

Although John Tunis referred to the "eleven wretched women" who ran the fateful 800-meter race at the 1928 Olympics, this photo shows only nine runners at the start. Lina Radke of Germany won the event in a world record time of 2 minutes, 16.8 seconds. *Both photos: The Bettmann Archive*

tape. I was informed later that the remaining starter fainted in the dressing room shortly afterward." Other accounts reported that all the women had finished the 800, but the impression of "eleven wretched women" was too vivid to erase. In 1929, the International Olympic Committee (IOC) voted to eliminate all women's track-and-field events from future Olympics, although they overturned the decision after the United States threatened to boycott the 1932 Games. Still, the 800-meter race was cut from the women's program. It was not reinstated until 1960.

For proof that properly trained women could handle an 800-meter race and more, Olympic officials had only to look at Eleanora Randolph Sears. In the first decades of the twentieth century, Sears was one of the most extraordinary of all athletes. A great-great-granddaughter of Thomas Jefferson, she was wealthy enough to spend a good deal of her time and money pursuing sports. Sears was an expert horseback rider, a great swimmer, and a national tennis champion in women's and mixed doubles. She raced powerboats and automobiles, and in 1910 she became the first Boston woman to fly an airplane solo. She played baseball, hockey, and golf, and organized her own football and polo teams. She also helped to make the game of squash racquets popular in the United States, winning the national championship and serving as captain of the U.S. international squash team. Of all her activities, though, the one that highlighted women's potential in

A true horse lover, Eleanora Randolph Sears rode for four hours almost every day. She also was a longtime financial supporter of the U.S. Equestrian Team and donated money to keep the National Horse Show an annual event. In 1957, she even donated horses and money to save the Boston Mounted Police. *Library of Congress, LC-B2-3821-5*

track and field was her marathon walking. In 1912, Sears took her first marathon walk, a 108-mile trek in California, which she completed in 19 hours, 50 minutes. She often walked the 47 miles from Providence, Rhode Island, to Boston, Massachusetts, clocking her best time of 9 hours, 53 minutes in 1926. On April 23, 1928, she set a new record by walking the 74 miles from Newport, Rhode Island, to Boston in 17 hours, 15 minutes. She covered an average of 4.4 miles per hour in a pounding rainstorm.

Eleanora Randolph Sears was a symbol of the positive values that sports brought to women's lives. But she also was the embodiment of a time gone by. Sears excelled at sports because she set personal challenges for herself, not because the public expected her to excel. With the rise of sports reporting in the 1920s and the growing debate about women and competition, sports could no longer be purely personal. The accomplishments of Sears, and Gertrude Ederle, and Ora Mae Washington, and Helen Wills inspired more girls and women to take up tennis rackets or golf clubs, to learn to swim or play ball. But as they ran and swam and won or lost, people were watching—and commenting. During the 1920s, women athletes became public figures, and all sorts of people now had a stake in what they did. Sports reporters built up players' rivalries to sell papers. Advertisers used pictures of women golf and tennis stars to sell products. Groups such as the AAU and the Women's Division fought a tug-of-war for the right to athletes' souls. For better or for worse, the Golden Age had brought women's sports into the big time, paving the way for bigger stars and new kinds of controversies.

In June 1921, Bessie Coleman became the first African American woman ever to earn a pilot's license. A stunt flyer and parachutist, she died on April 28, 1926, when the plane from which she was going to jump had mechanical difficulties and she fell to the ground. She was 34 years old.
The Bettmann Archive

Aileen Riggin, winner of the 1920 Olympic gold medal in women's springboard diving, displays her form at a New York aquatic carnival two years later. *Library of Congress Prints and Photographs Division*

The Women's International Bowling Congress held its first tournament in 1917. By 1923, Minnie Beringer, shown here, was one of the nation's top bowlers. She regularly scored higher than 200.
The Bettmann Archive

Glenna Collett Vare was largely responsible for the increased popularity of golf among American women during the 1920s. From 1922 to 1935, she won six U.S. Ladies Championships, and in 1924 alone she won 59 of the 60 tournaments that she entered. *UPI/Bettmann*

Women's baseball dates as far back as the 1860s, when students at Vassar played on a field away from public view. By the 1920s, a number of women's teams were traveling the country looking for games. In 1926, Peggy O'Neill, *above,* was a regular on an otherwise all-male team, the Tammany Tigers of New York. *The Bettmann Archive*

From 1920 through 1936, 265 women rode bucking broncos and roped and wrestled steers in professional rodeos across the United States. Historian Mary Lou LeCompte calls these cowgirls "pioneer professional athletes." This photograph shows an unidentified rider in action. *The Bettmann Archive*

Vacationers in Ocean City, New Jersey, take part in an early-morning calisthenics class in 1925.
UPI/Bettmann

1930 – 1945
All-American Girls

Mildred "Babe" Didrikson couldn't sleep the night before the 1932 AAU women's track-and-field championships. She'd traveled to Evanston, Illinois, to take part in the national meet, which also served as the trials for the 1932 Olympic Games. But instead of getting a good night's rest before the competition, Babe tossed and turned and suffered severe pains in her stomach. "When I put my hand on it, the hand would just bounce up and down," Babe remembered in her 1955 autobiography. The pain was so intense that she called the hotel doctor, who found her perfectly healthy except for a serious case of nerves. Babe took the news in stride. "I've found out since that whenever I get all keyed up like that before an event, it means I'm really ready."

Babe was in Evanston with her company team, Employers Casualty Insurance Company of Dallas, Texas. Actually, she *was* the team. Most of the other companies and sports clubs at the meet had sent 10 to 20 athletes, and in the open-

Babe Didrikson warms up for the javelin toss in a workout at the 1932 Olympics. In later years, Babe reacted to critics of her muscular appearance and aggressive behavior by softening her looks with makeup and feminine clothing. *AP/Wide World Photos*

ing ceremonies they stormed onto the field as their teams were introduced. After the public-address system announced Employers Casualty, Babe ran out alone, waving her arms to the cheering crowd. The spectators spurred her on. Babe was entered in eight of the meet's 10 events, and for three hours, she hurried from one to the next, running a heat in the 80-meter hurdles, then taking her turn at the high jump, then throwing the javelin or baseball or shot put. When the dust had settled, she'd won six gold medals, setting new world records in the baseball throw (272 feet, 2 inches), the javelin throw (139 feet, 3 inches), and the 80-meter hurdles (11.9 seconds). Babe had tallied 30 points, 8 more than the entire second-place Illinois Women's Athletic Club team. She'd single-handedly won the track meet in what United Press reporter George Kirsky called "the most amazing series of performances ever accomplished by any individual, male or female, in track-and-field history."

What made Babe Didrikson's showing in Evanston even more extraordinary was that until the track meet, her major sport had been basketball. Babe had taken a job with Employers Casualty right out of high school so that she could play basketball on the company team. In the 1920s and '30s, Babe's home state of Texas had a network of more than 40 company- or organization-sponsored women's basketball teams. Company coaches recruited high-school students the same way that college coaches recruit women players today. Employers Casualty paid Babe $75 per month as a secretary, even though she didn't know how to type when they hired her. The job enabled her to earn a living while still officially competing as an amateur athlete. But basketball season lasted only from January through March, and Coach M. J. McCombs didn't want his star athlete to get bored. To keep her active the other nine months of the year, he assigned Babe to the company softball and diving teams, had her play doubles in tennis, and trained her in track and field.

Babe's victories at the 1932 AAU championships won her a place on the U.S. team at the Olympic Games, held a few weeks later in Los Angeles. Although Babe had qualified for five of the six women's track-and-field events, a new rule, established after the 800-meter debacle at the 1928 Olympics, limited women to three events. Babe chose the javelin, the high jump, and the 80-meter hurdles, and she proceeded to better her performance at Evanston in all three. She threw the javelin 143 feet, 4 inches for a new world record and a gold medal. She ran the 80-meter hurdles in 11.7 seconds, also winning the gold and setting a world record. Then she tied U.S. teammate Jean Shiley with a world-record high jump of 5 feet, 5¼ inches, until the judges ruled that Babe dove over the bar headfirst, which was illegal. She argued that her feet had cleared the bar before her head, but the judges stood by their ruling and gave Shiley the gold. As a compromise, they allowed Babe and Shiley to share the new world record, and had a special second-place medal made for Babe that was half silver and half gold.

Babe's three world records made her the star of the Olympics, and her quick sense of humor made her a favorite with the press. After hearing that Babe played basketball, football, baseball, and many other sports besides running track, a *New York Times* reporter asked her, "Is there anything at all you don't play?" "Yeah," said Babe without missing a beat, "dolls." The answer helped earn her a new nickname, "the Terrific Tomboy." Others called her "the Texas Tornado" or simply "the Greatest Woman Athlete in the World." Sportswriter Grantland

81

Rice used Babe's accomplishments at the Olympics to argue that women had a bright future in track and field. "In spite of the many complaints about the awkwardness and out-of-place aspect of women in track-and-field sports, they have come a long way in a few years," Rice wrote in the September 24, 1932, issue of *Collier's*. He noted that women had set world records in all six of their track events at Los Angeles that summer. "Give them two or three more Babe Didriksons and most of the male athletes will be looking in the general direction of an exit."

Even with Rice's words of support, women's track and field continued to suffer criticism. In the 1920s opponents had claimed that women were too weak to perform well as track athletes. Now that Babe and others had proved them wrong, these same people charged that the sport

Babe turned professional at the end of 1932, trying her hand at many sports before settling on golf. Her decision was hastened by the AAU, which accused her of forfeiting her amateur standing by appearing in an ad for Dodge automobiles. Avery Brundage, then the AAU president, took the opportunity to belittle all women athletes, declaring, "You know, the ancient Greeks kept women out of their athletic games. They wouldn't even let them sit on the sidelines. I'm not so sure but they were right." *All four photos AP/Wide World Photos*

made women masculine, causing them to develop raw strength and muscles at the expense of their femininity. "I am fed up to the ears with women as track-and-field competitors," said U.S. Olympic Committee President Avery Brundage in 1936. "Their charms sink to less than zero." By the time Brundage made these remarks, Babe had left track and field, touring the country playing baseball, basketball, and a number of other sports before taking up golf. But the negative depiction of women track athletes as somehow not normal took its toll, as did the money problems that plagued track-meet organizers and company sponsors during the Great Depression of the 1930s. As the decade progressed, the AAU had an increasingly hard time finding sites for its women's indoor championships. Finally, the meet was canceled in 1937 and for the next several years.

At the same time that the AAU was turning its energies away from women's track and field, the African American community was rallying behind its female track stars. In 1929, Tuskegee Institute of Tuskegee, Alabama, formed one of the first women's college track teams in the United States, offering scholarships to promising female athletes and adding women's events to its Tuskegee Relays track meet. As early as 1930, newspapers in black communities encouraged girls and women to embrace track along with other sports. "Carefully checking school by school, playground by playground, Colored girls are showing a smaller percentage engaged regularly in athletic sports than any other race," noted Harry Levette, editor of the *California Eagle,* on March 14, 1930. "It is time to wake up and let's have some crack runners, swimmers, hurdlers, golfers, and other worthy stars in shades of brown and yellow. For after all, the athletic girl is the best looking and as a rule the most interesting."

Strength and speed were masculine characteristics to many leaders in the white sports world, but African Americans saw them as positive signs of determination and self-confidence. In the 1930s, black women became more and more visible in track and field, starting with Tidye Pickett of Chicago and Louise Stokes of Malden, Massachusetts, who won places on the 1932 Olympic team. But visibility and talent didn't guarantee these

Tidye Pickett trains for the Olympic hurdles trials at Randall's Island, New York, on July 8, 1936. *UPI/Bettmann*

women a chance to compete. After training to run the 400-meter relay at the Olympics, Pickett and Stokes were replaced at the last minute by two white runners who had not originally qualified for the U.S. team. This prompted the *Chicago Defender* to charge that "lily-whiteism," or racism, was "a thing more pronounced than anything else around [the Olympic Village] on the eve of the Olympic Games." Thirty-five years later, Stokes remembered, "A pretty fast stunt was pulled. This is what happened when we didn't have anyone to support us." Pickett and Stokes made the Olympic track team in 1936, but again Stokes was replaced in her event. Pickett, now a hurdler, made it all the way to the semifinals, where she hit a hurdle and was eliminated.

Tidye Pickett made history by becoming the first African American woman to compete in the Olympics, but her achievement was almost lost in the excitement over the Olympic men's track team, led by Jesse Owens. The 1936 Olympics took place in Berlin, Germany, three years after Nazi leader Adolf Hitler rose to power preaching a doctrine of anti-Semitism and racism. When Hitler's blond-haired, blue-eyed "Aryan" athletes went up against the racially mixed U.S. men's track team, they lost again and again. African American men won gold medals in six individual track events, including three won by Owens, who also anchored the gold-medal 400-meter relay team. His success was a direct challenge to Hitler and others who held that blacks were inferior to whites, and it encouraged African American men—and women—to try to follow in his footsteps. Soon black

The 1936 U.S. women's Olympic track team included two African Americans, Tidye Pickett, *front, third from right*, and Louise Stokes, *back, right. UPI/Bettmann*

women were becoming as dominant in track as black men. From 1937 through 1948, the Tuskegee women's track team won 11 of the 12 AAU outdoor track meets. By 1948, nine of the 11 members of the U.S. national women's track team were black.

African American track stars weren't the only women to gain new opportunities during the 1930s. The hard economic times brought about by the business failures of the depression had the unexpected effect of being a boon to sports. Starting in 1933, President Franklin Roosevelt introduced his New Deal, the set of programs meant to help the unemployed and revitalize U.S. business and agriculture. Among the New Deal programs was the Works Progress Administration (WPA), which hired out-of-work people to construct airports, bridges, hospitals, and a variety of athletic facilities. By the end of the decade, the WPA and other government agencies had built 3,600 baseball fields, 8,800 softball fields, and 13,000 playgrounds. Once these facilities were finished, the government provided funds so that cities could hire playground instructors to teach local children, and adults, how to play ball.

Thanks in part to this government support, softball grew overwhelmingly popular, ranking with bowling as

When women signed up to serve in the armed forces during World War II, they brought their love of softball with them. This team of Army nurses and Red Cross workers posed for a team picture in September 1943. *UPI/Bettmann*

one of the two top sports played by women in the 1930s. The Amateur Softball Association adopted official rules for the game in 1932, and the following year it held the first national championships for both men and women. Women competed on city teams, company teams, and even on teams formed at women's prisons. In 1938, a study reported that there were 1,000 women's softball teams in the Los Angeles area alone. On June 14, 1943, *Time* magazine estimated that there were 40,000 semipro women's teams across the United States, "sponsored by breweries, taverns, bakeries, big industries, and little individuals with a yen to see their names sprawled across the satin backs or sweatered fronts of cavorting U.S. tomboys." The best of these attracted women who were making softball their careers. Like Babe Didrikson, they took jobs with companies that fielded teams, earning money as secretaries or file clerks so they could play ball.

In 1943, Chicago Cubs owner Philip K. Wrigley offered these women the chance to leave secretarial work behind and become true professional athletes. As president of the William Wrigley, Jr., chewing-gum company, Wrigley had been a longtime sponsor of women's softball teams in California, and he was impressed with the talent and dedication that he saw. Early in 1943, he sent 30 of his baseball scouts to find the top ballplayers in the United States and Canada and invite them to try out for his new league. Wrigley invented a game that was part baseball and part softball, with nine players per team, base stealing, and a 40-foot pitching distance. (Softball teams usually fielded 10 players, outlawed stealing, and pitched 35 feet from the plate.) He felt certain that the media would soon agree that his women's game had "major league possibilities." Wrigley launched his creation, called the All-American Girls Softball League, with four teams in the spring of 1943. It became known as the All-American Girls Professional Baseball League after additional changes made the game more like baseball.

Wrigley was motivated by more than just his faith in women's softball. The United States had entered World War II in December 1941, and many of the nation's best major- and minor-league baseball players had joined or been drafted into the armed forces. At President Roosevelt's request, major-league ball would continue during the war. Yet Wrigley knew that fans would have little patience for the game played by the replacement players, men who were either too old or too young to be drafted. He felt that his women's league could preserve the spirit of baseball by offering high-quality, exciting games with the added appeal of the players' feminine charm. And he made sure that charm was easy to notice. Wrigley's players wore one-piece dresses as uniforms instead of the satin shirts and baseball pants worn by most female softball players of the day. During spring training in the first two years of the league's operation, they also attended special charm-school sessions, learning how to walk, sit, and speak with poise and class.

This emphasis on femininity reflected a growing concern about women's role in sports and in society at large. Not only were women athletes becoming stronger and more competitive, despite the best efforts of the Women's Division; women in general were now holding jobs that

Dottie Wiltse Collins went on to be one of the top pitchers in the All-American Girls Professional Baseball League, winning 20 or more games four times and ending her six-year career with a 1.83 lifetime earned run average. *Courtesy of the Northern Indiana Historical Society*

previously had been done only by men. By the summer of 1943, 10 million men were fighting overseas, and the U.S. Government needed women to rally behind them at home by building planes, driving buses, and running businesses. But while posters, songs, and newspaper editorials urged women to do their part to win the war, some people worried that women wouldn't want to give up their new jobs and power once the war was over. By presenting ballplayers who were skilled yet feminine, Wrigley reassured fans that he wasn't out to change the balance of power between men and women, and at least some fans were relieved. In May 1944, rookie pitcher Dottie Wiltse of the Minneapolis Millerettes received a letter congratulating her on her "splendid exhibition of pitching" in a recent game. "Frankly I was surprised at the talent which you girls have for the game," wrote Frank C. Schroder, who declared himself Wiltse's "favorite fan." He added, "I believe compliments are also in order for the very ladylike manner in which you girls acted while on the playing field. It was pleasantly surprising to say the least."

During the 1930s and '40s, the more seriously that women athletes approached their sports, the more concerned men were that they be "ladylike." Whenever possible, the media focused on the softer, more vulnerable side of athletic women, both in fact and in fiction. Articles about Wrigley's league regularly mentioned the players' legs, figures, makeup, and nail polish in the course of describing their baseball skills. A 1942 *Saturday Evening Post* feature on women softball players ended with writer Robert Yoder reassuring readers that "they may occasion-

These magazine covers from the 1930s reflect a growing concern, or at least a growing sense of humor, about women's changing roles in sports and society. *Collection of the author*

ally play like men, and occasionally even look like men, but beneath that satin perspiration shirt there beats a feminine heart." In fiction, sportswriter John Tunis created a strong female tennis champion in his 1940 novel, *Champion's Choice,* only to have her default in the middle of a Wimbledon final and go off to India with the man she loves. In film, 1941's *The Blonde Comet* followed a similar story line. This tale of a daring female auto racer ends when the woman is the front-runner at the Indianapolis 500, only to quit the race so the man she loves, a driver who has crashed, can borrow her car and win.

To many people, the women in these stories truly were "All-American Girls." They were talented, spunky, and clever, but not too proud or stubborn to know when to turn over the spotlight to their men. At a time when women athletes were making great strides and meeting increasingly difficult challenges, it was reassuring to think that, deep down, these athletes were typical American girls. But there was nothing typical about a hurdler who could cover 80 meters in under 12 seconds, or a catcher who could whip the ball into second base to catch a runner stealing. The women athletes of the 1930s and early '40s were stronger and smarter and better trained than ever before. They also were more dedicated to sports and to competition. These athletes, in Philip Wrigley's league and everywhere else, were helping to create a new "All-American Girl." And this one wouldn't leave a race until it was over.

From 1927 through 1936, Norway's Sonja Henie dominated the sport of figure skating, winning 10 consecutive world championships and gold medals at three Olympic Games. Then, she took Hollywood by storm in a string of movies that featured her skating. Henie's success in competition and in films helped to increase the popularity of ice skating in the United States. *Collection of the author*

Lillian Copeland, shown here practicing the shot put, was one of America's first female track-and-field stars. Copeland took the gold medal in the discus throw at the 1932 Olympic Games. *Library of Congress, LC-USZ62-078589*

"Strongwoman" Relna Brewer shows off her physique on the beach at Venice, California, on November 22, 1937. By the 1930s, fitness advocates were already linking beauty and athleticism. In the August 1929 issue of *Physical Culture* magazine, publisher Bernarr Macfadden told readers, "The real source of beauty and charm is found deep within the body itself. And a woman who craves these rich possessions should adhere to a routine of body building." *UPI/Bettmann*

In 1931, 17-year-old pitcher Virne Beatrice "Jackie" Mitchell struck out New York Yankee greats Babe Ruth and Lou Gehrig in an exhibition game. Mitchell, a pitcher with the Chattanooga Lookouts Class AA minor-league team, was the second woman ever to sign a minor-league contract. The first, Lizzie Arlington, pitched for two Pennsylvania teams in 1898. *The Bettmann Archive*

1 9 4 6 – 1 9 6 5
Ladies Through and Through

T oni Stone dug her cleats into the dirt, cocked the bat, and waited for the pitch. This was no ordinary at bat. The pitcher, Satchel Paige, was one of the best ever to take the mound. He'd been throwing for close to 30 years, mostly in the Negro leagues, which had developed after organized baseball banned African Americans at the end of the nineteenth century. Stone was the only woman to play at the top level of the Negro leagues, covering second base in 1953 for the Indianapolis Clowns and in 1954 for the Kansas City Monarchs. On this day, Easter Sunday, 1953, Paige was taking a break from his duties with the major-league St. Louis Browns. And he was in familiar form. "He was so good that he'd ask batters where they wanted it, just so they'd have a chance," Stone told author Barbara Gregorich years later. When he put that question to Stone, she shrugged and answered, "It doesn't matter. Just don't hurt me." The big right-hander wound up, lifting his front foot so that his shoe was all Stone could see. "I stood

99

there shaking," she said, "but I got a hit. Right out over second base." It was, she admitted, the happiest moment of her life.

Stone's meeting with Paige was the high point in a baseball career that started when she was growing up in St. Paul, Minnesota. From as early as she could remember, Stone loved baseball. She played whenever she got the chance, and hung around the baseball school started by former major-league catcher Gabby Street until he gave her a tryout. Street was so impressed that he bought her a pair of cleats and welcomed her as a student. At the time, Stone was playing under her real name, Marcenia Lyle, but people started calling her Tomboy. When she moved to San Francisco to play ball during World War II, Tomboy changed her nickname to Toni and added the last name of Stone. She joined a men's barnstorming team, which traveled around the country taking on various opponents along the way. Then she made it into the Negro minor leagues, and finally into the Negro majors with the Clowns and the Monarchs.

Despite the widespread acceptance of female track athletes in the African American community, Toni Stone's achievements in baseball were looked upon with some suspicion. Instead of competing in a sport with only women, Stone was playing with and against men, under their rules and on their turf. She did a respectable job, batting .243 in 50 games in 1953. But the following year, when the African American magazine *Jet* ran an article on "The Truth About Women Athletes," it reported that officials at a "Southern Negro college" awaited a guest

After Toni Stone quit baseball at the end of the 1954 season, she returned to the Oakland, California, home that she shared with her husband, Aurelious Alberga, and worked as a nurse. She is shown here in a 1953 publicity photo. *National Baseball Library & Archive, Cooperstown, New York*

appearance by Stone with much anxiety, "expecting the worst after hearing many disconcerting rumors about women athletes." They breathed a collective sigh of relief when she got there. "Miss Stone arrived in a pink flowered dress, enthralled the campus with her feminine charm and grace, and shocked those who expected a muscular, harsh-voiced mannish woman," the magazine reported on August 5, 1954. "In conversation, Toni Stone spoke in a well-modulated, girlish voice [and] seemed more interested in fashions, cooking, and homemaking than in batting averages, double plays, and bench jockeying."

Jet's assessment of Stone, and its satisfaction at finding that, deep down, she was "a lady through and through," is a sign that concerns about the femininity of women athletes had spread from the white to the black community by the 1950s. This was due at least in part to the overwhelming pressure on women to return to their roles as homemakers following the end of World War II. National leaders who had called for women to work in factories during the war suddenly urged them to quit their jobs so that returning soldiers and sailors could take their places. Almost overnight, the independent women who had kept the war effort going on the homefront went from being admired to being criticized. Businesses helped to open up jobs for men by firing women in large numbers. By the end of 1946, more than two million women had lost their jobs at airplane factories, shipyards, and in other "heavy" industries. Magazines ran articles suggesting that it was now a woman's patriotic duty to help her husband take over as the family breadwinner. "All the average man asks," wrote the editor of the *Ladies Home Journal* in December 1945, "is that his wife and/or sweetheart be a sturdy oak while he's away at war or the office and a clinging vine on his return."

This changing attitude about women's role in society affected the way that Americans looked at women athletes and women's sports. Sports that emphasized "feminine" qualities, such as grace and beauty, continued to be acceptable for women, but those that depended on outright shows of strength or endurance, or even on cooperation between teammates, had an image problem to overcome. It was fine for women to be figure skaters or gymnasts or, better yet, cheerleaders who used their athletic talents to support men's teams. But if women could play baseball or basketball like men, how could they be "clinging vines" who gave up everything for their husbands? And if they didn't give up everything for their husbands, how could they be real, or normal, American women? Ironically, the journalists and social critics who wanted to contain or limit women's sports began to sound a lot like the leaders of the Women's Division, who had objected to competition for female athletes since the 1920s. Yet the Women's Division leaders also wanted to give every girl and woman the power over her own athletic destiny. These postwar social critics had no interest in giving women any sort of power. Instead, they helped to bring about a backlash that threatened to slow down or even reverse the progress that women in sports had made.

Baseball was one casualty of this new femininity. Toni   **103**

Stone retired from the game after the 1954 season, and the All-American Girls Professional Baseball League folded that same year, leaving no women in professional baseball and little hope of future baseball opportunities for women. Across the nation, there was a growing feeling that women should play softball, which had been invented with women in mind, and leave baseball to the men. On May 26, 1952, *New York Times* television reporter Jack Gould wrote a column about a televised women's baseball game that left no question about his feelings on this matter. The Saturday night contest featured two amateur teams: the Amazons, of Summit, New Jersey, and New York's Arthur Murray Dancers, sponsored by dance-studio owner and instructor Arthur Murray. "The Arthur Murray Dancers are the home team and they are such a comely nine that it is difficult to believe that they cannot get dates on Saturday night but must play baseball," wrote Gould. "It hardly seems the best advertisement for [Mr. Murray's] dance studio that a young lady should have to slide into second. Shouldn't she know the rapture of the heavenly waltz in the arms of the man who took advantage of the free, easy lesson? Whose side is Mr. Murray on?"

Some women athletes did survive the postwar backlash without becoming the objects of ridicule or sarcasm. As the nation struggled to guarantee African Americans their civil rights, black women athletes in particular saw their

Phyllis Riggs of Ohio State University leads a cheer for her team at a 1952 football game. Two years later, in a wrap-up of the major sports events of 1954, *Sports Illustrated* included no women's events and showed women only as cheerleaders. *UPI/Bettmann*

Professional baseball opportunities for women disappeared after the All-American Girls Professional Baseball League folded in 1954. During better times, in 1948, a hustling Faye Dancer slides into third to avoid the tag of Marge Wenzell. *Courtesy of the Northern Indiana Historical Society*

opportunities and successes increase. At the same time that Toni Stone broke barriers by competing with men, other African American women were winning the right to compete on equal terms with white women. In 1948, Alice Coachman of Albany, Georgia, continued the Olympic tradition started by Tidye Pickett and Louise Stokes and became the first African American woman to win an Olympic gold medal. Coachman, a graduate of Tuskegee Institute, set a new Olympic record in the high jump with a winning leap of 5 feet, 6⅛ inches. In 1960, 20-year-old Wilma Rudolph of Clarksville, Tennessee, captivated a worldwide television audience when she won Olympic gold medals in the 100-meter and 200-meter sprints and then anchored the 400-meter relay team for another gold.

LADIES THROUGH AND THROUGH

Rudolph was the first American woman to win three gold medals in track and field at one Olympics.

In 1950, 23-year-old Althea Gibson did what Ora Mae Washington, Lucy Slowe, and other great African American tennis champions couldn't; she got the chance to prove herself against all opponents, black and white. In August of that year, Gibson became the first African American to play in the United States Lawn Tennis Association's National Championships at Forest Hills, New York. She was two games away from a second-round upset victory over Wimbledon champion Louise Brough when a thunderstorm forced the match to be postponed. Play resumed the next day, but by then Gibson had lost her momentum and Brough squeaked by with a victory,

In a warm-up for the Olympics, Alice Coachman clears the bar at 5 feet to win the high jump at the 1948 National AAU women's track meet. *AP/Wide World Photos*

6–1, 3–6, 9–7. Gibson followed Forest Hills by playing a tournament in Miami, Florida, becoming the first black to enter a formerly all-white tennis competition in the Deep South. "I'm an authority on what it feels like to be the only Negro in all-white surroundings," she said afterward, "and I can assure you, it can be very lonely." The following summer, she added another first to her résumé, journeying to England to become the first black player to enter Wimbledon.

Although Gibson continued to earn respect on the tennis circuit, the lifestyle took its toll. In the 1950s, most tennis tournaments were for amateurs only. The U.S. Nationals and Wimbledon offered trophies instead of prize money, and players either had to pay their own expenses or depend on backers who could afford to support them. Althea Gibson had grown up without much money, and was initially helped out by two African American doctors who saw her potential as a future champion. After four years on the tennis circuit with no major wins, she grew uncomfortable depending on others. "I'm just not good enough," she recalled thinking in her autobiography, *I Always Wanted To Be Somebody.* "I'm probably never going to be. I'm sick of having people support me, taking up collections for me, buying me clothes, and airplane tickets, and every damn thing I eat or wear. I want to take care of myself for a change."

As a child, Wilma Rudolph contracted pneumonia and scarlet fever, diseases that caused her left leg to be paralyzed. The story of how she overcame this disability to become the world's fastest woman was chronicled in the 1977 TV movie *Wilma.* Here, Rudolph is about to break the tape to win the 400-meter relay for her team at the 1960 Olympic Games. *AP/Wide World Photos*

Gibson took time off to teach physical education and considered joining the Army, but before she did, a new coach convinced her to give tennis one more try. This time, she achieved the success that had eluded her. In 1957, Gibson won the women's singles and the women's doubles titles at Wimbledon and defeated Louise Brough in the finals at Forest Hills to take the U.S. National title too. "Shaking hands with the Queen of England was a long way from being forced to sit in the colored section of the bus going into downtown Wilmington, North Carolina," she wrote in her autobiography. "Dancing with the Duke of Kent was a long way from not being allowed to bowl in Jefferson City, Missouri, because the white customers complained about it." As if to prove that her year at the top wasn't a fluke, Gibson won all three titles again in 1958. Then she retired from amateur tennis. She remained the only African American U.S. or Wimbledon champion until Arthur Ashe won the U.S. Open in 1968 and Wimbledon in 1975.

When Gibson did quit tennis, she briefly turned to golf as a way to stay in sports and make money at the same time. Although there were few professional women's tennis tournaments until the late 1960s, a year-round circuit of professional women's golf tournaments was up and running by the early 1950s. Actually, the history of professional golf for women goes back farther than that, to the Women's Professional Golfers Association (WPGA), founded in 1944. This group disbanded before the end of

On the way to her first Wimbledon singles title, Althea Gibson reaches for a shot by England's Christine Truman in their July 5, 1957, semifinal match. *AP/Wide World Photos*

the decade, but it had one lasting effect. When the founders of the new pro golf tour met to hammer out the details in 1949, they learned that they couldn't legally use the name of the old group. Instead, they called their organization the *Ladies* Professional Golf Association (LPGA), over the objection of several players. Using the word "ladies" was like sewing "a strip of lace on the title," complained golfer Betty Hicks. Aware of the need to cast women golfers as feminine and "normal," that might have been exactly what the founders had in mind.

Moonlighting as a journalist, Betty Hicks did her part to help shape the image of her sister golfers. In a January 23, 1954, article for *The Saturday Evening Post,* Hicks gave readers a thorough introduction to the players on the LPGA circuit, as well as revealing behind-the-scenes details of life on the tour. The article, titled "Next to Marriage, We'll Take Golf," also emphasized the importance of marriage and family to the golfers. "Most of the single pros admittedly are keeping one eye on the ball and the other peeled for a likely prospect to lure them from the circuit to the altar," wrote Hicks. Then she quoted Betsy Rawls, the tour's top money winner in 1952, who, Hicks said, was sure to become the LPGA's number-one star "unless she meets her man, which is more than likely." According to Hicks, Rawls declared, "There's only one thing that could be more fascinating than golf. That would be raising children."

Originally the script for *Pat and Mike* called for Katharine Hepburn's Pat, *right,* to beat Babe Didrikson in a golf match, but Babe said she wouldn't make the movie unless she won. In the film, Babe wins by one stroke on the eighteenth hole and walks off the green surrounded by adoring fans. *UPI/Bettmann*

Spencer Tracy gives his star athlete encouragement during her workout in *Pat and Mike*. UPI/ *Bettmann*

LADIES THROUGH AND THROUGH

If the LPGA tried a bit too hard to impress fans with the femininity of its athletes, it was not alone. Rather than questioning or confronting the public's need to fit female athletes into comfortable, acceptable slots as wives or mothers, most sports followed the golf association's lead. One of the few attempts to take a deeper look at a woman athlete's motivations was made not by journalists or social commentators, but by filmmakers. The 1952 romantic comedy *Pat and Mike* cast Katharine Hepburn as an all-around athlete named Pat Pemberton and Spencer Tracy as Mike Conovan, a sports promoter who becomes her manager. The film uses real-life athletes as Pat's competitors, and Hepburn performs all of Pat's athletic feats herself. She is shown golfing against Babe Didrikson and Betty Hicks, among others, and playing tennis against stars Alice Marble and Gussie Moran. But Pat has a tendency to choke in the middle of a match, and with Mike's help she comes to realize that it happens whenever she makes eye contact with her fiancé, a college president who disapproves of her competitive lifestyle. This man, a "likely prospect" by most women's standards, causes Pat to feel and play like a loser. Instead of marrying him and quitting sports, Pat breaks her engagement and immediately starts to win matches. When she falls in love with Mike at the end, theirs is a more equal relationship, with Mike admitting that he needs her as much as she needs him.

Pat and Mike was pure entertainment, although anyone looking to use it as a jumping-off point for a debate on women and sports could find plenty to talk about. At the same time that Hepburn was showing her athletic prowess in movie theaters, a more curious group of entertainer-athletes was attracting its own share of attention. They were the men and women of Roller Derby, a form of sports entertainment that brought out the best—and worst—in American sports fans, and broke a lot of rules about femininity in the process. Roller Derby was the brainchild of Leo Seltzer, a businessman who in 1935 was looking for a way to profit from America's fascination with roller skating. The first Roller Derby was an endurance contest. Male-female pairs took turns skating a total of 4,000 miles as fast as they could. Within a few years, though, Seltzer came up with a better idea. He put together two teams with ten skaters each, five men and five women, and had the teams skate for points instead of distance. Both teams sent five-member "packs" onto the track at the same time, women against women or men against men. Two of the skaters on each team, called jammers, tried to break out of their pack and pass their opponents to score points. At the same time, two other team members, called blockers, tried to stop the opponent's jammers by pushing them or knocking them off their feet.

Roller Derby enjoyed a period of popularity before World War II, but its real boom started in November 1948, when television discovered the sport. Television was still new in 1948; Americans owned only about 600,000 sets at the beginning of the year. The few television stations in operation didn't always have enough programs to fill their schedules, so when Seltzer's skaters came to New York City for 17 matches, he was able to talk CBS into broadcasting some of them live. People who had never heard of Roller Derby suddenly found themselves sitting in their living rooms watching this strange phenomenon. They stared frozen in amazement as men and women punched each other, tripped each other, and pushed each other over the guard rails. It was like a wrestling match on wheels, and these new fans couldn't get enough. The night before the first TV broadcast, only 200 spectators came out to see the Derby in

Roller Derby superstar Midge "Toughie" Brasuhn tries to skate past Julie Patrick, *in helmet. Library of Congress Prints and Photographs Division*

person. After the first broadcast, fans stormed the arena and jammed phone lines, and Seltzer sold as many as 7,000 tickets per match for an arena that usually seated only 5,600. Newspapers ran front-page articles on the Roller Derby, and its male and female skaters became famous overnight.

At a time when Americans were obsessed with the femininity of their women athletes, the popularity of the rough-and-tumble female Roller Derby skaters seems hard to explain. In his 1971 book about the Derby, *Five Strides on the Banked Track,* sportswriter Frank Deford suggested that cheering for or against the skaters helped frustrated fans deal with the pressures in their own lives. He quoted Jerry Seltzer, who took over the Derby from his father, Leo, in 1958, as Jerry pointed to a woman in the stands. "Sometimes I think we must be doing a service," Jerry said. "I think we must be keeping that woman from going home and killing her husband tonight. And every night there is some woman like that."

For their part, the women skaters found that in the 1950s and '60s, Roller Derby was one of the best ways for a female athlete to earn a living. Superstar Joanie Weston once hit .730 as a softball player, but there was little money in that. Skater Earlene Brown won a bronze medal in the shot put at the 1960 Olympics, but that didn't pay the bills. Roller Derby wasn't refined like golf or tennis. Skaters risked injury every time they entered the track, but in a way, that was part of the appeal. The opportunity to go all

Monta Jean Payne of the Jersey Jolters, *in white shirt,* slams Toughie Brasuhn into the rail during another 1950 Roller Derby match. *Library of Congress Prints and Photographs Division* out, to use strength, skill, and cunning, and have crowds rooting madly for or against you made Roller Derby the most liberating women's sport of its time. The Derby rode several waves of popularity, right up to the early 1970s. Only then, as women started to win the right to participate more equally in mainstream sports, did the fortunes of the Roller Derby begin to fade.

Skier Gretchen Fraser became the first American woman to win a gold medal at a Winter Olympics when she placed first in the slalom in 1948. Fraser also took home a silver medal in the alpine combined event. *UPI/Bettmann*

Swimmer Esther Williams was all set to go to the Olympics in 1940 when they were canceled due to World War II. Instead, she took part in an aquacade, or water show, and was "discovered" by talent scouts from MGM. During the late 1940s and early '50s, Williams swam her way through a dozen films, including *Million Dollar Mermaid*, a 1952 hit in which she played former swimming sensation Annette Kellermann. *Collection of the author*

In 1951, Betty Chapman of Glencoe, Illinois, became the first African American to play professional softball. Chapman was an outfielder for the Admiral Music Maids of the Chicago-based National Girls Baseball League (NGBL). Despite its name, the NGBL played softball, not baseball. *UPI/Bettmann*

Often called the "Jackie Robinson of tennis," Althea Gibson offers tennis tips to the baseball star himself at a celebrity tournament in 1951. *AP/Wide World Photos*

1 9 6 6 – 1 9 8 1
A New Era

Billie Jean King was on a plane from Japan on May 13, 1973, but her mind was on a tennis match being played in California. The match pitted 30-year-old Australian Margaret Smith Court against 55-year-old Bobby Riggs, the 1939 Wimbledon singles champion who was waging a one-man campaign to show that men's tennis was superior to women's. At a time when many women in the United States were fighting for equal rights under the banner of women's liberation, Riggs prided himself on being a Male Chauvinist Pig, a man who claimed that women didn't deserve equal rights because they were inferior to men. Riggs declared that any male tennis player could beat any female player, and that the women's game was less interesting than the men's. He said that women tennis players shouldn't earn the same money as men because a woman couldn't win more than a game or two against a man. Riggs set out to prove his point by challenging King to a match. When she said no, he challenged Court, the only active female player to have won a grand slam, having taken the Australian, French, Wimbledon, and U.S. Open singles titles in 1970.

By the time Billie Jean King's plane stopped to refuel in Hawaii, the Riggs–Court match was history. The over-the-hill chauvinist seemed to prove his point by burying Court 6–2, 6–1. When King heard the score, she "went bananas," according to her 1974 autobiography, *Billie Jean*. "Right then and there I said, 'That's it. I've got to play him,'" King wrote. "The door had been opened and things were out of my control." King felt that Court's loss might lead people to believe Riggs's claim that women's tennis was dull, and keep them from supporting the newly established women's professional tennis tour. Just three years before, in 1970, King and eight other players had broken away from the male-dominated pro-tennis circuit to play a tournament of their own. In 1971, Virginia Slims cigarettes had signed on as the major sponsor of a series of 14 women-only tournaments, each with at least $10,000 in prize money. The women's tour continued to grow, but it depended on fans to come to matches and root for the players. Without fans, the sponsors might pull out.

Riggs contacted King about a follow-up match before she had the chance to get in touch with him. Their match was set for September 20, 1973, to be played in the Houston Astrodome and telecast live during prime time over ABC. While Riggs and Court had played for a prize of $10,000, King and Riggs would compete for $100,000, winner take all. Each player also was guaranteed at least $75,000 from endorsements and souvenir sales. The meet-

Bobby Riggs already seems to be showing the strain as he arm-wrestles Billie Jean King at the July 12, 1973, press conference announcing their upcoming "Battle of the Sexes." *UPI/Bettmann*

ing was quickly dubbed the "Battle of the Sexes," and Riggs did his best to focus the nation's attention on it, traveling from city to city to give interviews and meet the public. By contrast, King played her regular schedule of tournaments and then withdrew to South Carolina to practice and work on a game plan. "Each of us treated the match very differently," King wrote in her autobiography. "I was deadly serious about it; for him it was the ultimate ego trip, a vehicle for a super hustler to carry off (he hoped) the ultimate hustle."

There was so much hype for the match that on the day

it was to be played, *The New York Times* declared, "By any stretch of the imagination, this three-of-five set match has become the most talked-about event in the history of tennis." More than 28,000 people paid from $6 to $100 each for tickets to the match and more than 48 million tuned in on TV. King entered the stadium on a regal chair carried by five muscular male athletes, while Riggs entered in a carriage pulled by six scantily clad female models. It seemed more like a circus than a sports event, until the tennis began. Then all of King's preparation paid off. She was in control of the match from the start, playing her

Billie Jean King enters the Houston Astrodome carried by "gladiators"—really track athletes from Rice University—for her September 20, 1973, match against Bobby Riggs. *UPI/Bettmann*

serve-and-volley game and tiring Riggs out by running him all around the court. King won the first set 6–4, taking 26 of her 34 points on all-out winners, shots that Riggs never even touched. She won the second set 6–3 and the third by the same score. The entire match took 2 hours, 4 minutes. Afterward, an exhausted Riggs admitted, "She was too good. She played too well."

Billie Jean King's victory over Bobby Riggs struck a symbolic blow for women's liberation and for women's sports. It wasn't that women wanted to play against men, but rather that they wanted respect as athletes and opportunities to earn their livings at their sports. There was no reason King *shouldn't* have beaten Riggs. He was as old as her father and his finest moments in tennis had taken place around the time that she was born. But the fact that King stood up under pressure and won the match in straight sets seemed to wake people up to women's athletic potential. The day after her victory, *New York Times* tennis writer Neil Amdur compared King's achievement to those of Joan of Arc, the fifteenth-century French military hero. "There can be no doubt that Mrs. King's triumph, viewed by so many, has strengthened her [position] as the Joan of Arc of athletics," wrote Amdur, "the one who raised her racquet for battle when few women challenged the broad inequalities inherent in the sports structure."

While the King–Riggs match was a turning point for women's sports, it was just one of the breakthroughs that took place during the 1960s and '70s. The changes started with a major policy shift. At the 1960 Olympic Games, **129**

Wilma Rudolph's triple-gold-medal performance showed millions of television viewers that America's female athletes could be the best in the world if they received the proper training and support. Rudolph was a student at Tennessee State University, one of the African American schools that had helped to keep competition for women alive after the Women's Division ruled against it in the 1920s. Her success, along with prodding from the United States Olympic Committee, finally moved the Women's Division to reverse its policy. By 1963, the women's group had voted to endorse intercollegiate women's sports and to encourage coaches to train promising athletes for international events. In 1971, the leaders of women's college sports went one step further. They formed the Association for Intercollegiate Athletics for Women (AIAW), to plan, govern, and promote the growing number of college tournaments for female athletes.

Women also began to fight for the right to compete in sports outside of school. On April 19, 1967, 20-year-old Kathrine Switzer made the directors of the Boston Marathon fighting mad when she became the first woman to officially enter the 26-mile, 385-yard race. The Boston Marathon was strictly a men-only affair, so Switzer hid her gender until the race was under way. She signed her

Two miles after the start of the 1967 Boston Marathon, race director Will Cloney, *in dark coat and hat*, tries to snatch the cardboard number from Kathrine Switzer's chest. Switzer, *number 261*, breaks away from Cloney with the help of her running partner, Tom Miller, *number 390*. Then Boston Athletic Association trainer Jock Stemple, *in dark jacket*, runs after her, but he too is pushed away by Miller. The Boston Marathon finally invited women to enter in 1972, giving in to a protest that began with the publication of these photographs. Switzer was one of nine women to finish the race that year. *UPI/Bettmann*

application "K. Switzer," asked her male teammates from Syracuse University to pick up her number at the sign-in table, and started running in a hooded sweatshirt. After she pushed back the hood and race organizers saw she was female, they tried to tear the cardboard number from her chest and force her off the course. Later, race director Will Cloney explained that international rules barred men and women from running in the same race, and that the AAU limited women's distance races to 1½ miles. "I am hurt to think that an American girl would go where she is not wanted," said Cloney, the father of three daughters. "If that girl were my daughter, I would spank her." Switzer, who finished the race in 4 hours, 20 minutes, said she ran because it made her "feel strong, all there." She added, "I think it's time to change the rules. They are archaic. Women can run, and they can still be women and look like women."

Soon after Kathrine Switzer defied officials of the Boston Marathon, younger athletes around the country began an assault on a group that was strictly boys-only, the Little League. The Little League's charter stated that it was a boys' organization whose purpose was to instill manhood through baseball. In July 1971, when Little League Manager Donald Sciuto allowed 12-year-old Sharon Poole to play for the Haverhill (Massachusetts) Indians, he was fired and she was kicked off the team. In the spring of 1972, when 12-year-old Maria Pepe joined the Hoboken (New Jersey) Young Democrats, the Little League's national headquarters threatened to withdraw their sponsorship of her team and every other one in

Maria Pepe, shown here in 1974, played three Little League games with the Hoboken Young Democrats before she was forced off the team. By the time the Little League changed its policy to include girls, Pepe was too old to play. *UPI/Bettmann*

Hoboken. In June 1973, when 12-year-old Carolyn King won a place on the Ypsilanti (Michigan) Orioles, her manager got a call informing him that the Orioles would lose sponsorship too. Poole, Pepe, and King went to court over the right to play ball, and they weren't the only ones. By March 1974, girls and their parents in 15 states, including future major-league Manager Dallas Green and his nine-year-old daughter Kimberly, had filed lawsuits against the Little League. On September 7, 1974, the organization finally agreed to ban sex discrimination on all of its local teams. Instead of instilling manhood, its new goal would be to teach players to be good citizens and good sports.

As the 1970s progressed, the courts played an increasingly important role in opening up new athletic opportunities for girls and women. Despite the Women's Division's change in policy, most public schools still shied away from competition for female students, instead spending practically all of their sports money on boys. In 1969, the Syracuse, New York, school board earmarked $90,000 for boys' high-school teams and set aside only $200 for girls'. At the college level, the numbers were even more dramatic. In 1973, the University of Washington budgeted $1,300,000 for men's programs, not including football and basketball, and $18,000 for women's programs. Public schools and colleges were using tax dollars in a way that discriminated against female athletes, a practice that defied state and federal laws. With a growing awareness of the potential benefits of sports for girls, parents' groups and athletes began to take their school boards to court. In state after state, they won rulings that directed schools to start girls' teams or let girls compete with boys. "There is no fundamental right to engage in interscholastic sports," wrote Judge Genevieve Blatt in a 1975 Pennsylvania ruling. "But once the state decides to permit such participation, it must do so on a basis which does not discriminate."

Athletic equality got a big boost from these court decisions, but it was the U.S. Congress that shifted reform into high gear. In 1972, Congress passed the Education Amendments to the 1964 Civil Rights Act. Title IX of these amendments held that schools receiving money from the federal government could not discriminate against any person on the basis of sex. Schools that didn't comply would risk losing their federal funds. Almost all U.S. schools and colleges received some federal money, and almost all of them discriminated against female students by offering males vastly superior sports programs. Besides sponsoring more boys' teams than girls' teams, schools tended to save the best playing fields for boys, assign them more convenient practice times, buy them nicer uniforms, and pay their coaches higher salaries. Female athletes in college found many of the same inequalities, with one important addition. In the early 1970s, U.S. colleges awarded scholarships to approximately 50,000 male athletes each year. The total number of women receiving athletic scholarships was less than 50.

Title IX was celebrated by supporters of women's sports and attacked by those who worried that more opportunities for women would mean fewer ones for men. Leading the opposition was the National Collegiate Athletic Association (NCAA), the group that governed men's college sports. The NCAA complained that Title IX would destroy men's sports programs by draining their funds. The group argued that big-time college football and basketball programs, some of which earned millions of dollars for their schools, should not have to comply with Title IX. NCAA lobbyists went to Congress to try to stall the writing of guidelines for carrying out this new law, and their efforts worked. Guidelines were not issued until 1975, and secondary schools and colleges were given until

1978 to upgrade their programs. Even after that deadline, the NCAA and individual schools continued to protest Title IX, taking their fight all the way to the Supreme Court. In 1984, the Court interpreted the law in a way that excused most sports programs from complying, but in 1988, Congress restored the original intent of Title IX. When a more conservative political climate resulted in a change of leadership in the House and Senate in 1994, efforts to overturn Title IX began anew.

Despite the NCAA, Title IX brought about widespread changes in school and college sports for girls. In 1970, 294,000 high-school girls took part in interscholastic sports. By 1978, that number had increased to 1,600,000. In 1972, the average college spent less than 2 cents of every dollar of its athletic budget on women's sports. By 1980, that average had risen to 16.4 cents. Women's sports scholarships were up too, from only a handful in 1973 to approximately 10,000 in 1978. So were championship tournaments for women. By the end of the 1970s, the AIAW offered 41 national women's tournaments and more than 700 state and regional tournaments.

All of these numbers added up to a revolution in women's sports, but the revolution wasn't just about numbers. It was about college athletes such as basketball star Ann Meyers, winner of the first sports scholarship awarded to a woman by UCLA. A four-time All-American, Meyers

In 1979, Ann Meyers became the first woman ever to sign a contract with a team in the National Basketball Association. The Indiana Pacers guaranteed Meyers a salary of $50,000, but she ended up working in the front office instead of playing ball. She had more success with the New Jersey Gems of the Women's Professional Basketball League, winning honors as Most Valuable Player during her first season there. *UPI/Bettmann*

helped the United States win a silver medal at the first women's Olympic basketball competition in 1976, and then led the UCLA Bruins to their first women's national championship in 1978. It was about amateur athletes such as Linda Jefferson, halfback for the Toledo (Ohio) Troopers, a women's football team. Jefferson, who juggled a midnight-to-four A.M. job and a full load of college courses to make time for football, beat out a long list of more well-known athletes as the *womenSports* magazine readers' choice for 1974 Athlete of the Year. The women's sports revolution also was about sports reporters such as Melissa Ludtke of *Sports Illustrated.* Tired of waiting outside New York Yankee locker rooms while male reporters went inside, Ludtke sued major-league baseball for the right to interview players at the same time as her male colleagues. In 1978, a U.S. District Court judge ruled that all reporters, male or female, should have the same access to athletes, in locker rooms and everywhere else.

On the heels of the revolution in women's sports came increased recognition for female athletes. There was a lot of room for improvement. Between August 1972 and September 1973, NBC televised 366 hours of live sports. Just one of those hours was devoted to a women's event, the Wimbledon tennis final. The following year, CBS did only slightly better than its rival network, devoting 10 of its 270 hours of sports programming to women. Print coverage was just as spotty. Most local newspapers rarely reported the results of area high-school or college women's games, and when national magazines paid any attention at all to female athletes, they seemed to focus

Peanuts creator Charles Schulz was a big supporter of women's tennis and other women's sports. This 1982 cartoon is a virtual *Who's Who* of women athletes of the day, from speed-skaters Beth Heiden and Sarah Docter to bowler Donna Adamek and marathoner Allison Roe (Schulz spelled her name wrong). *PEANUTS reprinted by permission of United Feature Syndicate, Inc.*

more on their looks and personal lives than on their athletic performances. Billie Jean King once refused to do a photo layout for a women's magazine after the photographer asked her to pose lying across a couch in a slinky dress. When she founded *womenSports* magazine in 1974, she wrote, "*WomenSports*, I hope, will not only give women athletes the coverage they deserve, but will cover them as athletes who happen to be women, not as decorations or sideshow attractions in the real world of sports."

Unfortunately, the history of women's sports in the United States was bound up too much with the issue of femininity to allow female athletes to be evaluated solely on **139**

"Pound for Pound, You're as Good as He Is."

womenSports

is about joy, activity, Olga Korbut, equal prize money, motorcycling, Virginia Slims, photography, jogging, leotards, the Olympics, surfing, pushups, menstruation, Babe Didrikson, eight-

ball, softball, Roller Derby, isometrics, backgammon, back trouble, backpacking, the basic woo position, nutrition, sports during pregnancy, sports and ageing, drag racing, sky diving, poker, bingo, competition, machismo, "femininity," feminism, day care, skin care, circulation, aikido, clubs, gyms, gymkhanas, hang gliding, Olga Connolly, pro-ams, The Atoms, Esther Williams, racquet ball, hand ball, pin ball, water polo, discus throwers,

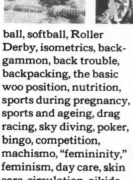

Sonja Henie, muscles, teeth, fat, cellulite, paunches, punches, self-defense, karate, ballet, Robyn Smith, cartoons, platform shoes, sports fashions, slot machines, fun, Howard Cosell, ping pong, massage, rolfing, hotdogging, winning, training, weightlifting, figure skating, backhand grips, acrobatics, osteo-pathy, Martha Graham, water skiing, volley ball, modern dance, Dinah Shore, Jean Balukas, Denise Long, Princess Anne, Evonne Goolagong, the Bauers, the Bundys, the New York Fillies,

color, Gertrude Ederle, Donna de Varona, Australia, suntans, health, lady wrestling, wrist wrestling, laughing, wet suits, sports groupies, gambling, drugs, scores,

records, statistics, humor, Olympics sex tests, Doctor Tenley Albright, men, jocks, slaloms, tournaments and you.

Read about you in

womenSports

This ad from the first year of *womenSports* magazine promises subscribers the chance to read about the people and issues that matter to them as athletes and sports fans. The ad reflects the magazine's sense of humor and spirit of empowerment. *Collection of the author* the playing field. The old distrust of women who were strong and independent had survived the 1950s, and now the critics of women athletes pulled no punches. "This is kind of how it is," LPGA golfer Jo Ann Prentice told *Sports Illustrated* in 1973. "If you get into town at the beginning of the week and you meet some guy whose company you enjoy and have dinner with him once or twice, the gossips start asking what kind of tramps are these babes on the tour. If you stay at the motel where everybody else on the tour has checked in, then the question is what are those girls doing back in those rooms alone." Women who were passionate about sports drew the suspicions of people who were threatened by their talent. The assumption that female athletes were somehow immoral, throwing themselves at men or at other women, was a handy way to dismiss their accomplishments. Aggressive, competitive women had no place in the narrow definition of femininity that these people adhered to. Rather than marvel at their athletic abilities, these critics sought ways to discredit them.

Homophobia was behind many of the remarks about the character of women athletes. Detractors were quick to imply that an athlete was lesbian by describing her as "mannish" or "masculine." Such comments served to force lesbian athletes to hide their sexuality and younger women, both lesbian and heterosexual, to avoid sports altogether out of fear of being labeled gay. This robbed lesbian fans of potential role models and cheated the sports world out of potential champions. It also allowed people who were uncomfortable with the subject of homosexuality to avoid questioning their feelings about it.

Fittingly, it was Billie Jean King who finally made the public come face-to-face with homosexuality, although this time her pioneering was not by choice. In 1981, King's former secretary, Marilyn Barnett, filed a lawsuit seeking money and property that she said King had promised her during their long lesbian affair. On May 1, King faced the media with her husband, Larry, beside her and admitted that she had, indeed, been involved with Barnett. In the days that followed, reporters conducted what one athlete called a "gay witch hunt," speculating in print on the role of lesbianism in women's sports. The *National Enquirer* went so far as to offer tennis players $5,000 if they would name names. The athletes refused, saying that what people did in their private lives was private. When King volunteered to step down as president of the Women's Tennis Association (WTA), the players' labor union that she had organized in 1970, the women on the tennis tour refused to accept her resignation.

Only a few months after King's press conference, Martina Navratilova publicly admitted her own bisexuality. Yet these revelations did not lead to an open dialogue on homophobia in women's sports. Athletes knew that their sports depended on the companies that sponsored them, and no sponsor wanted to be identified with a subject that made the public uncomfortable. This lesson was brought home at Wimbledon in July 1982. After a tumultuous year, including a legal victory over Marilyn Barnett, 38-year-old Billie Jean King surprised everybody by making it all the way to the semifinals. Throughout the tournament, King wore the same outfit, an old tennis dress devoid of any sponsors' logos. After she lost her semifinal match to Chris Evert, *Sports Illustrated* explained why King had appeared in the old outfit. In the year since admitting her lesbian affair, King had lost an estimated $1,500,000 in endorsements, including her clothing contract. The symbol of the new era in women's sports had paid the price with the shirt off her back.

Figure-skater Peggy Fleming's elegant style on the ice won her a gold medal at the 1968 Winter Olympics. She would go on to star in her own NBC special, skate professionally, and become a familiar spokesperson in TV commercials. *Collection of the author*

Cathy "Cat" Davis, *left,* started boxing to keep in shape, but found that she had a talent for the sport. Here, she takes a right from Germany's Uschi Doering. Davis, the women's lightweight boxing champion, went on to win this 1979 bout in the sixth round on a technical knockout. *UPI/Bettmann*

One of the best softball pitchers of all time, Joan Joyce of the Raybestos Brakettes gets ready to burn one in and lead her team to their first World Women's Softball Championship, on August 17, 1974. *UPI/Bettmann*

On May 22, 1977, Janet Guthrie, a 39-year-old physicist, rejoiced after becoming the first woman ever to qualify for the Indianapolis 500. A few days later, this cartoon commemorated her accomplishment. Mechanical difficulties would cause Guthrie to pull out of the race after 27 laps, but she came back in 1978 to finish ninth against 33 male drivers. *Photo, UPI/Bettmann; cartoon, Bob Englehart/Copley News Service*

147

In 1978, Nancy Lopez was the LPGA Rookie of the Year, winning nine tournaments and earning $189,813, a record for any rookie golfer, male or female. Here, she blasts a shot out of the sand on the ninth hole of the Colgate–Dinah Shore Winners Circle Golf Championship on April 7, 1979.

AP/Wide World Photos

Diane Crump, *center*, becomes the first woman in U.S. thoroughbred-racing history to compete in a regular event, on February 7, 1969. She rides Bridle'n Bit to a tenth-place finish in a 12-horse field. *UPI/Bettmann*

Wyomia Tyus, *breaking the tape*, followed in the footsteps of Wilma Rudolph when she won the gold medal in the 100-meter sprint at both the 1964 and 1968 Olympics. She also won a third gold and a silver medal as part of two U.S. relay teams. *AP/Wide World Photos*

1 9 8 2 – T O D A Y
Taut, Toned, and Coming On Strong

Fourteen minutes into the final game of the 1995 NCAA Division I women's basketball championships, the undefeated University of Connecticut Huskies were in trouble. Two of UConn's top players, forward Rebecca Lobo and point guard Jen Rizzotti, already had three fouls. Another key player, center Kara Wolters, had two. If any of these All-Americans was called for another foul before halftime, UConn was almost certain to lose. Coach Geno Auriemma made sure that didn't happen by benching Lobo and Wolters until the third quarter. He told the remaining players, led by forward Jamelle Elliott, to try to keep the score close. As the 18,000 fans in the Minneapolis (Minnesota) Target Center looked on, Elliott and freshman guard Nykesha Sales did just that, allowing the University of Tennessee Lady Volunteers only a six-point advantage at halftime. When they returned to the court, Lobo and company came back in force, matching Tennessee basket for basket and even slowly chipping away at their lead. 151

UConn tied the score with 2 minutes, 17 seconds to go, and then Rizzotti grabbed a rebound and flew down the court to sink a layup. With 1 minute, 51 seconds left, the Huskies took the lead for good. At the final buzzer, UConn won the game and the championship, 70–64, finishing the season with a record of 35 wins and no losses.

As the Huskies celebrated their perfect season, supporters of women's sports cheered the new degree of enthusiasm for women's basketball. The UConn–Tennessee final was played on Sunday afternoon, April 2, 1995, but the tickets to the game had been sold out since September 1994. The CBS national telecast of the women's final beat its competition, attracting more viewers than the National Basketball Association (NBA) games on NBC and almost three times as many viewers as the National Hockey League (NHL) games on Fox. Some people predicted that this was just the beginning. "You think you've seen growth in women's basketball," broadcaster and former All-American Nancy Lieberman-Cline told *The Sporting News*. "Wait until you see what happens the next five years." For starters, ESPN had just paid $19 million for the exclusive rights to show the women's NCAA tournament through the year 2002, and the cable network planned to broadcast as many as 31 tournament games in 1996. "ESPN is going to promote the heck out of this," said Lieberman-Cline, "and make the names of players and coaches become household words."

University of Connecticut forward Carla Berube, *right*, collides with Tennessee center Dana Johnson as she passes the ball during the first half of the NCAA women's basketball championship title game on April 2, 1995. Tennessee's Michelle Marciniak, *3*, looks on. *AP/Wide World Photos*

Women's basketball had been on the verge of becoming a major sport in the United States for close to 20 years, since Lieberman-Cline and Ann Meyers helped to raise the level of the game in the late 1970s. But many women thought one of the first leaps forward for the game actually was a step backward. During the 1970s, the female-run Association for Intercollegiate Athletics for Women (AIAW) had overseen the tremendous growth of college basketball and other women's college sports. In 1981, the NCAA started to challenge the AIAW by offering its own national women's championships in some sports. Since the NCAA had fought Title IX so vehemently, AIAW leaders didn't trust the group's motives. They warned that the NCAA was interested in women's competitions only because of the additional money that Title IX would pump into women's programs. The AIAW sued to try and keep the NCAA out of women's sports, but in 1982, the NCAA went ahead with its plans to hold its own Division I women's basketball championships. When 17 of the top 20 teams chose the NCAA's tournament over the one sponsored by the AIAW, leaders of the women's group realized they were fighting a losing battle. By the time the AIAW lost its lawsuit in 1984, the group had shut down altogether.

Although women gave up a measure of control over college sports when the NCAA came into power, they also gained prestige. Their sheer numbers even forced some male athletes, administrators, and fans to take the presence of women in sports more seriously. From the early 1970s to 1990, the number of women playing college sports jumped from 16,000 to 160,000. By 1994, one third of all college athletes were female. Outside of school, the increase was just as dramatic. During the 1980s alone, the number of female tennis players soared from 4,000,000 to 11,000,000, and as a fitness craze swept the nation, millions of women started running, bicycling, and joining gyms. On August 30, 1982, *Time* magazine ran a cover story on "the new ideal of beauty," one that included a body that was "taut, toned, and coming on strong." According to journalist Richard Corliss, "As a comely byproduct of the fitness phenomenon, women have begun literally to reshape themselves, and with themselves, the American notion of female beauty." Gail Eisen, co-author of a book on physical conditioning, told Corliss, "Just being thin isn't pretty anymore. Now beauty is the vibrancy of someone who's got blood rushing through her body from exercise. To be beautiful you have to be healthy. And to be healthy you have to exercise."

Women who exercised could take their inspiration from athletes such as Mary Lou Retton, Martina Navratilova, and Jackie Joyner-Kersee, who personified the new fitness of body and spirit. At the 1984 Summer Olympics in Los Angeles, Retton bounded over the vault, bounced through the floor exercises, and danced across the balance beam, dazzling the world with her strength and grace. The 16-year-old West Virginian came away with two bronze medals, two silvers, and the first-ever U.S. gold medal for women's gymnastics, in the all-around competition. Navratilova's speed, power, and finesse redefined women's tennis, and her training regimen of weight-lifting, **155**

1984 Olympic gymnastics gold medalist Mary Lou Retton shows her strength and poise on the balance beam. *UPI/Bettmann*

computer-generated workouts, and a low-fat, high-carbohydrate diet set a new standard for women in all sports. Her intense rivalry with Chris Evert brought out the best in each player and gave fans an enduring lesson in how to combine respect and sportsmanship with all-out competition. After taking a silver medal in the heptathlon at the 1984 Summer Olympics, Joyner-Kersee came back to win the gold in both 1988 and 1992, earning praise from sports commentators who called her "the greatest athlete in the world." Among the many awards Joyner-Kersee received for her athletic and humanitarian accomplishments, perhaps the most telling was the *Glamour* magazine Woman of the Year, a sign that taut muscles had indeed become "glamorous" for American women.

Before the 1980s, most women who played sports had to make do with clothing and equipment originally designed for men. As greater numbers of women turned to sports, a host of products sprang up to meet their needs, many of them developed by other women. In 1978, runner and costume designer Hinda Miller became increasingly frustrated with the flimsy, everyday bras that offered little

A study in mutual respect, Martina Navratilova, *left*, and Chris Evert leave the court after the 1983 U.S. Open final. Navratilova won in straight sets, 6–1, 6–3. *UPI/Bettmann*

support as she ran mile after mile. She and her partner solved the problem by sewing two jockstraps together to make a stronger garment that cut down on bounce by holding the breasts closer to the chest. Their invention, refined to become the JogBra, gave birth to the $30 million sports-bra industry. In the mid-1980s, researchers at Brooks running shoes learned that 42 percent of the 30,400,000 runners in the United States were female. Brooks sponsored a study to find out whether women runners were different from their male counterparts, and the results surprised them. "Women run on the inside soles of their feet more often than men," reported Eric Dryer, head of research and development at Brooks. He added that women also have more flexible joints than men, and the proportions of their bodies are different, all of which adds up to the need for special shoes. In 1987, Brooks brought out the Devotion, the first running shoe entirely designed for women. Soon after that, every major running-shoe company followed their lead.

Advances in clothing and equipment helped make women more viable competitors in all kinds of sports. So did a general change in attitude. For much of the twentieth century, women athletes had to fight against society's definition of what was "feminine" to play most sports. But the feminists of the 1970s encouraged women to become physically fit. In September 1973, *Ms.* magazine declared that by developing physical strength, a woman "will inherit the essential source of human self-confidence—

Jackie Joyner-Kersee gets astounding height as she leaps to a 22'7" victory in the long jump at a May 16, 1987, track meet. *AP/Wide World Photos* pride in and control over a finely tuned body." By the 1980s, women who had heeded this advice were moving into positions of power in business, government, and other areas of American life. A 1994 survey by *Women's Sports and Fitness* magazine found that 82 percent of the most powerful female politicians in Washington had taken part in organized sports when they were young. And the new generation of girls and young women assumed it was their right to play sports. "I've never seen women as strong, as well developed," Donna Lopiano told *The New York Times* in 1982. Lopiano, the director of women's athletics at the University of Texas, would go on to become executive director of the Women's Sports Foundation. "They arrive here [at the university] outgoing, confident, with a good self-image," she continued. "It's beginning in their hometowns, where athletic scholarships have become status symbols. They're not hiding in their rooms with people saying, 'Oh, those phys-ed majors.' They're like male athletes. They're revered."

Physically fit and self-confident, women in the 1980s and '90s took on increasingly difficult challenges in all types of sports. When she read about the first Iditarod Trail Sled Dog Race in 1973, 19-year-old Susan Butcher set her sights on this 1,100-mile dogsled competition from Anchorage to Nome, Alaska. She became a veterinarian's assistant, learned to train and breed sled dogs, and finally, in 1978, felt ready to enter her own dog team. Butcher finished every Iditarod through 1984, sometimes placing as high as second, and was leading the race in 1985 when a moose attacked her team, killing two dogs and injuring 13.

On June 23, 1987, President Ronald Reagan and Senator Ted Stevens of Alaska, *right*, enjoy the message on a sweatshirt commemorating the second straight Iditarod victory of Susan Butcher, *left*. *UPI/Bettmann*

That year, Libby Riddles became the first woman ever to win the Iditarod, but for the rest of the 1980s, the race belonged to Butcher. She placed first in 1986, 1987, 1988, and 1990, setting a course speed record in 1990 of 11 days, 1 hour, 53 minutes, and 23 seconds. In 1989, the *Anchorage Times* named her the Sled Dog Racer of the Decade.

Erin Whitten went to her first ice-hockey tryout when she was eight years old, and despite coming home with blisters on her feet from skates that were two sizes too small, she was hooked. Fourteen years later, on October 30, 1993, Whitten became the first female goalie credited with a win in (men's) minor-league hockey, leading the Toledo (Ohio) Storm of the East Coast Hockey League to a 6–5 victory over the Dayton (Ohio) Bombers. That season,

Goaltender Manon Rheaume uses her glove to make a save during her professional debut with the Tampa Bay Lightning of the NHL on September 24, 1992. Rheaume gave up two goals in one period during an exhibition game against the St. Louis Blues. *AP/Wide World Photos*

Whitten was one of three female goalies in hockey's minor leagues. Kelly Dyer was in the net for the West Palm Beach (Florida) Blaze. Canadian Manon Rheaume, who a year before had had a much-publicized tryout with the Tampa Bay Lightning of the NHL, played with the Nashville (Tennessee) Knights. In 1993, a total of 269 women played on organized ice-hockey teams in the United States, not including those on the women's teams at 40 U.S. colleges. The following year, Minnesota became the first state to approve girls' ice hockey as a high-school varsity sport. In 1998, women's ice hockey will become a medal sport at the Winter Olympics in Nogano, Japan.

Not all of the inroads made by ground-breaking athletes in the 1980s and '90s took place on ice and snow. Girls' and women's soccer experienced a boom in the United States that started with the growth of youth soccer leagues in the late 1970s and hit new heights when the U.S. women's team won the first-ever women's World Cup in 1991. This time period also saw an enormous increase in women's college teams. From 1982 to 1995, the total number of NCAA colleges with women's soccer teams grew from 80 to 446, making it the largest intercollegiate soccer network in the world. The United States had no professional soccer league for women, but an amateur women's league launched in May 1995 started with 19 teams based across the country. And on the eve of the 1996 Summer Olympics in Atlanta, Georgia, officials started noticing a curious trend. Though tickets entitled spectators to see both a men's and a women's Olympic soccer match on the same day, many ticket buyers indicated that they were interested only in seeing the women.

While sports participation by girls and women in the United States increased tremendously, newspaper and television coverage of their accomplishments continued to lag behind. A 1990 study by the Amateur Athletic Foundation of Los Angeles (AAF) broke down the sports news found in four major U.S. daily papers over a period of three months. The study found that men's sports received 81 percent of the coverage, women's sports received 3.5 percent, and the remaining 15.5 percent focused on neutral topics, such as the sites of future Olympic Games. A 1989 AAF study of television coverage found that 92   **163**

percent of TV sports featured men, 3 percent featured women, and 5 featured neutral topics. As before, a good deal of the coverage that women athletes did receive had little to do with their athletic achievements. In the February 20, 1994, edition of *The New York Times*, columnist Linda Truman Ryan reviewed the covers of *Sports Illustrated* that showed women in the 52 weeks from February 1993 to February 1994. There were six women pictured in all. One was a swimsuit model and two were the wives of baseball players who had been killed in a boating accident. The other three were athletes who were the victims of violence. Tennis-player Monica Seles was stabbed by a fan of rival Steffi Graf. Tennis-player Mary Pierce was harassed and beaten by her father. Figure-skater Nancy Kerrigan was attacked by men hired by the ex-husband of opponent Tonya Harding.

One reason for this imbalance was the fact that most sportswriters and sports editors were men. In 1994, author Mariah Burton Nelson reported that in the United States, only four sports editors and about eight percent of sportswriters and broadcasters (about 800 out of 10,000) were female. But those numbers were slowly on the rise. In 1993, Cassandra McAboy was hired as the only woman, other than the secretary, in the 16-person sports department of the *Mobile* (Alabama) *Register*. McAboy was assigned to cover college football, but she also wrote a lot about gender issues and local girls' and women's

American Michelle Akers takes control of the ball in the 1995 World Cup semifinal match between the United States and Norway. Akers led the U.S. team to their 1991 victory in the first women's World Cup. *Chris Cole/Allsport* teams, and she traveled to Minneapolis to cover the 1995 NCAA women's basketball championships. "You can imagine how many female sportswriters I see in Alabama, in the South, period," said McAboy. "I got to Minneapolis and I said, 'Holy cow!' I never knew there were so many women in this business." Even at an event where most of his colleagues were women, a male reporter at a pregame press conference asked a group of UConn players a question that suggested he wasn't the best person to cover women's sports. Referring to the huge shopping mall near Minneapolis, he asked, "It's a given that women love to shop. Have you been to the Mall of America yet?"

If there is a difference between the articles women and men write about female athletes, it may be that many women tend to focus on the athletes' motivations as well as their achievements. By humanizing the women they portray, these writers help to provide role models for girls who are hungry for heroes. "My 10-year-old daughter reads *Sports Illustrated*," wrote Lynda Truman Ryan in her review of the magazine's covers. "Her ritual is to flip through the pages looking for two things—baseball, and anything, anything at all, about girls. I wish the editors had the imagination to think of her." When the University of Connecticut won the NCAA women's basketball championship in 1995, *New York Times* reporter Abby Goodnough called the players "graceful athletes who have become role models for girls across [Connecticut]." Kathy Carroll, whose eighth-grade daughter played on a

basketball team, told Goodnough, "My daughter watches

them and says, 'I wish I could play like that. I hope I can do that well.' They inspire her."

Thanks to the ever-expanding universe of cable television, young women in the 1990s could look forward to watching more and more female athletes on TV. In 1994, two separate groups announced plans to launch women's sports networks with round-the-clock coverage of professional, college, and high-school women's competitions, as well as exercise and nutrition programs. And existing cable channels, such as ESPN and ESPN2, continued to increase the attention they paid to women's events. At the broadcast networks, ABC led the way in 1994 with a documentary on women's sports, to the credit of Lydia Stephans, vice president of programming at ABC Sports. After Stephans first proposed the documentary, the men who sold advertising on her network's sports shows told her they couldn't find a single company willing to pay to air commercials on a program about women. Stephans was amazed, until she found out that the salesmen had asked only the advertisers who sponsored ABC's male-oriented sports shows, companies that made razors, after-shave, trucks, and the like. Stephans opened the eyes of her salesmen by seeking commercials from the advertisers on ABC's entertainment and daytime shows, companies that made products for women. In the end, she was so successful that *A Passion to Play* turned into a series, with eight shows from 1994 through 1996.

Ultimately, the female athletes whom girls and women read about or see in action will be responsible for even

greater growth in women's sports. The power of role models to inspire future athletes is that great. Witness the effects of the movie *A League of Their Own,* Penny Marshall's fictionalized version of the first year of the All-American Girls Professional Baseball League. *League* premiered in July 1992 to mixed reviews, but the reception it got from female viewers of all ages helped to make it one of the highest-grossing films of the year. And its impact went far beyond the box office. Soon after the movie opened, women from all walks of life started wearing baseball shirts as a fashion statement. Within weeks, television commercials for everything from soft drinks to cold remedies showed women playing baseball or softball. More important, a number of promoters started planning new professional opportunities for women in these sports. In 1994, the first of these efforts, the Colorado Silver Bullets all-female professional baseball team, barnstormed the country playing against men's semipro and minor-league teams. In 1995, the National Baseball Hall of Fame announced plans to expand its exhibit on women in baseball due to overwhelming popular demand. In the spring of 1996, Spalding Sports introduced the first baseball glove specifically designed for women, whose hands are typically 15 percent smaller than men's hands.

As women become increasingly proficient in sports, they will begin to command the respect of even their most skeptical opponents. It's already happened with the Silver Bullets. In July 1995, the Bullets were scheduled to play

Colorado Silver Bullets pitcher Gina Satriano gets ready to deliver the ball. *Otto Greule/Allsport* the men's team at a U.S. Air Force base. Concerned that his men might lose to the women, the Air Force manager flew in unauthorized players from other bases to assure a victory. When Bullets Manager Joe Niekro found out about these ringers, the Air Force was forced to forfeit the game. If a team of women athletes can turn back the most powerful air force in the world without a fight, the future of women's sports seems limitless indeed.

Women's volleyball surged in popularity during the 1980s and '90s. In this 1987 match, the University of Hawaii's Mahina Eleneki spikes the ball past Stanford's Wendi Rush as Hawaii wins its third NCAA Volleyball Championship. In 1994, a nationwide study of more than 14,000 Americans found that women made up 55 percent of the nation's court volleyball players. *UPI/Bettmann*

Kristi Yamaguchi skates her way to another U.S. gold medal in figure skating at the 1992 Olympics in Albertville, France. *Reuters/Bettmann*

In 1984, the Olympics finally offered women the chance to run distances longer than a mile. Joan Benoit of the United States literally ran away with the first Olympic women's marathon, finishing in 2 hours, 24 minutes, and 52 seconds. Harkening back to the women's 800-meter race from 1928, TV coverage followed up the report on Benoit's triumph by showing a Swiss runner who finished thirty-seventh, in pain and "delirious." *UPI/Bettmann*

Janet Evans raises her arm in victory after winning the gold medal in the 400-meter individual medley at the 1988 Olympics. Evans won two other swimming gold medals in 1988, and another in 1992. *Reuters/Bettmann*

At the 1984 Olympics, Evelyn Ashford became the first American since Wyomia Tyus to win the gold medal in the 100-meter sprint. She also anchored the U.S. 4 × 100-meter relay gold-medal team, and is shown here winning the semifinal heat. *AP/Wide World Photos*

At the 1994 Winter Olympics, speed-skater Bonnie Blair won two gold medals and increased her total to five gold and one bronze, collected over three different Olympics. Before Blair, no American woman had won more than four gold medals at either the Winter or the Summer Games.

Reuters/Bettmann

The America³ team's *Mighty Mary* is ahead of the *Stars & Stripes* in 1995 America's Cup yachting action. The America³ crew was the first all-female America's Cup yacht-racing team ever, although a male navigator was added late in the competition. *Reuters/Bettmann*

THE POWER AND
THE PROMISE

In the spring of 1973, *Sports Illustrated* published a ground-breaking, three-part report by journalists Bil Gilbert and Nancy Williamson on the state of women's sports in America. Toward the end of the report, the authors predicted what would happen if the number of girls and women competing in sports increased greatly. "Sports previously thought too 'difficult' or 'physical' for girls may be opened to them," they wrote. "The demand for coaches and trainers, as well as for equipment specifically designed for females, will increase. In time, women's sports will attract greater public interest. The press will cover women's athletics more frequently and seriously. Sports heroines will be discovered. Women's professional sports will become more popular, more lucrative and thus more attractive in career terms."

Gilbert and Williamson were on target in every one of their predictions. Today girls and women are taking part in the roughest, toughest sports, everything from boxing to ice hockey. There no longer is a category labeled "too difficult for girls." There are more coaches and trainers for women, and as mentioned earlier, there are now running shoes, sports bras, and even baseball gloves designed just for them. The gradually increasing press coverage has resulted in a larger following for women's sports, higher prize money, and new career opportunities. And yes, the public is discovering new female sports heroes—from the present and the past—every day. The very attitude of girls and women toward sports has changed. Now it's second nature for a girl to play softball or soccer and to set her sights on a college athletic scholarship. Girls used to treat sports as a privilege, something they needed permission to do. Today they treat it as a right.

Still, the liberation of women's sports is not complete. According to the NCAA, in 1992, colleges and universities spent only 20 percent of their athletic budgets on women's sports and offered female students only 28 percent of their athletic scholarships. And as the number of women athletes in colleges has increased, the number of women coaches has dwindled. The enhanced status of women's college basketball and certain other sports has led to more visibility and sometimes higher coaches' salaries, making the job of coaching women more appealing to men. In the early 1970s, 90 percent of women's college teams had female coaches, but in 1990, only 47.3 percent of women's college teams were coached by women.

There are other issues as well, one of the most impor-tant of which is safety. Women who exercise outdoors often fall victim to annoying comments, harassment, or

Women's sports came a long, long way during the 101 years that separate these portraits of female tennis players. The *Girl with Tennis Racket* in A. S. Seer's 1887 drawing hardly looks like she was able to bend down, let alone smash an overhead. Chris Evert, on the other hand, proved that she could do it all, winning 157 singles titles and earning eight year-end number-one rankings during her eighteen-year career. *Drawing, Library of Congress, LC-USZ62-15750; photograph, Reuters/ Bettmann*

worse. A 1983 survey of 100 members of a Washington, D.C., women's running group found that 41 reported having been threatened by one or more men while running. In September 1995, a New York woman who had been jogging in Central Park became the latest statistic when she was assaulted, beaten, and killed. The next morning, radio disk jockeys criticized the victim for jogging alone in the dark. There was still an assumption that women should curb their athletic activity and that, if they didn't, no one could be responsible for what happened to them. In 1990, this attitude and various assaults against women runners and walkers led the Road Runners Club of America to launch a program of Safety Summits, which aimed to reduce crime against women who exercise outdoors. The summits include seminars with FBI agents and police offi-

Soccer wasn't much of a contact sport when the Whites, *with white sashes*, played the Blues in this 1914 game. By the time the United States, *in white*, met Japan in the 1995 World Cup quarterfinals, neither team held anything back. The United States won this match, then lost to Norway in the semifinals. *1914, Library of Congress, LC-USZ62-33738; 1995, Chris Cole/Allsport*

Perfectly posed and perfectly poised, this 1912 girls' basketball team from Monroe, Wisconsin, seems to have a solidarity born of loyalty and teamwork. By contrast, two 1996 USA Olympic basketball stars are more animated about the game they love: Sheryl Swoopes in a Nike poster and Rebecca Lobo (overleaf) after her UConn team's 1995 NCAA victory. *1912, Library of Congress, LC-USZ62-37433; Swoopes, courtesy of Nike; Lobo, Matthew Stockman/Allsport*

cers who educate women athletes on how to maintain their safety without sacrificing their workouts.

Homophobia also continues to threaten the ability of all women to enjoy sports. On May 13, 1995, Valerie Helmbreck of *The* (Wilmington, Delaware) *News Journal* reported that CBS golf analyst Ben Wright told her that "lesbians in the sport hurt women's golf," specifically because corporate sponsors don't want to be associated with the "butch" image that these women project. Although Wright denied the comments, the article set off a wave of speculation on women athletes, lesbianism, and

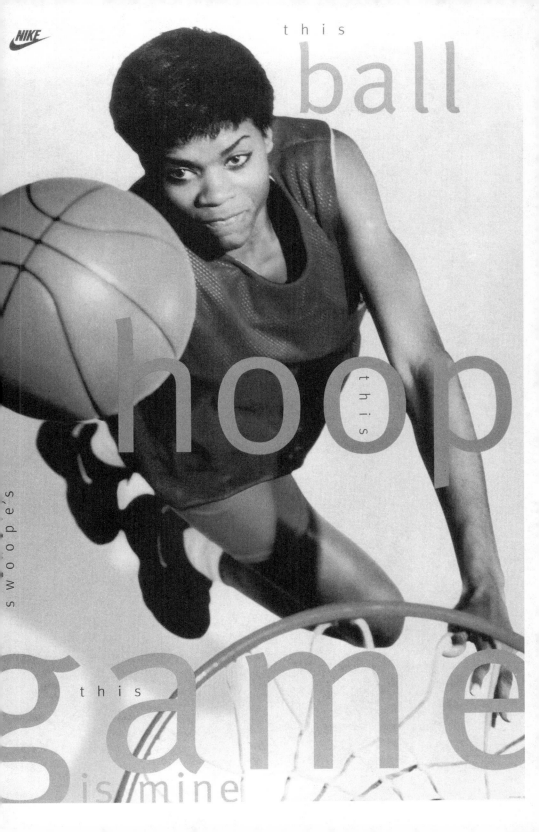

femininity similar to the one after Billie Jean King's 1981 press conference. Women golfers were quick to condemn Wright's words, but his bosses at CBS initially believed his claim of innocence and signed him to a new four-year contract. In January 1996 CBS finally pulled Wright off the air after he admitted making "insensitive remarks" to Helmbreck. For its part, the LPGA says that no corporate sponsor has ever cited lesbianism as a reason for withdrawing its support. But the image of its golfers is a big concern to the LPGA, so much so that the golf tour employs a fashion consultant who travels with the players from tournament to tournament. In his reaction to the Wright affair, *New York Times* columnist Ira Berkow took issue with this emphasis on appearances. Berkow suggested that, for once, it would be nice to have an open panel discussion on image, lesbianism, and femininity in women's sports—and he suggested that it take place on CBS. As of this writing, no one has picked up on the suggestion.

Despite the issues still to be resolved, sports are transforming American women. Instead of just enjoying basketball and tennis and mountain climbing and skating for the sheer physical experience, women are starting to use the values and attitudes they have developed in these sports to get ahead in other areas. It turns out that loyalty, determination, competition, and teamwork are as important in government and the business world as they are on the athletic field. "Sports were where I learned respect for the rights of others, even when I wanted to defeat them," Florida Congresswoman Carrie Meek told *Women's Sports*   **187** *and Fitness* magazine in December 1994. "I fought tough battles, and I learned that being behind didn't necessarily mean losing—there's always a chance to come back and win." In 1986, sociologist Gai Ingham Berlage surveyed 168 fathers whose daughters played competitive soccer. When she asked whether they thought their daughters' soccer experience would be an advantage in a business career, 89 percent answered yes. The fathers cited compromising, handling pressure, and discipline as sports lessons that would be useful in business. One father, a corporate director, told Berlage, "The goal orientation, competitiveness, and team concepts of competitive sports have direct parallels in business."

Of course Frances Willard knew that more than a century ago. When she wrote, "I began to feel that myself plus the bicycle equaled myself plus the world," she was expressing, in nineteenth-century terms, the power and the promise that sports hold out to every woman and girl. During the past 150 years, no matter what the prevailing opinion was of their role in society, women have sought out that promise. Whether they swam the English Channel, sprinted into the record books, or hit home runs for the war effort, they acted on their need to test their limits, feel strong and comfortable in their bodies, and compete. As the girls and women of the twenty-first century pursue their own dreams of glory, they will be well served to look back at the pioneers who sweated it out before them. It is their winning ways that will make it possible for the trailblazers of tomorrow to take women's sports to a new and even higher level.

C H R O N O L O G Y
Firsts, Records, and Other Noteworthy Events

📷 *Indicates that a photograph related to this item or individual appears in the book.*

The 1800s: A Century of Progress

1856: Catharine Beecher publishes *Physiology and Calisthenics,* possibly the first fitness manual for women. 📷

1873: *September 6:* Ten women compete in a mile swimming race in New York's Harlem River. Delilah Goboess of Philadelphia wins the first prize, a $175 silk dress.

1874: Mary Ewing Outerbridge introduces tennis to the United States. 📷

1876: *November 17–19:* Mary Marshall, a 26-year-old marathon walker, wins two out of three 20-mile races against Peter Van Ness in New York. The contest is billed as the first sports competition between the sexes without a handicap. Marshall's prize is $500.

1878: *December 16:* Madame Ada Anderson begins her month-long marathon walk in Brooklyn, New York, and ushers in a rash of pedestrian contests for women.

1879: Twenty women enter the National Archery Championship, the first national tournament for American women in any sport.

1881: Bell Cook and Emma Jewett attract as many as 20,000 spectators at a time as they tour the United States challenging each other to 20-mile races on horseback.

1883: *June 16:* The New York Gothams of the National Baseball League sponsor the first "Ladies' Day," inviting women to see that day's game for free.
Also: Mrs. M. C. Howell wins her first archery title. From 1883 to 1907 she would win the national women's archery championship 17 times.

1885: Sharpshooter Annie Oakley signs on as the first cowgirl in Buffalo Bill's Wild West show. She would become the first female Wild West superstar.

1891: *March 27:* Zoe Gayton arrives in New York City 213 days after leaving San Francisco, walking the entire way and averaging 18 miles per day. She wins $2,000 plus as much as $10,000 in side bets.
Also: YMCA instructor James Naismith invents basketball.

1892: Gymnastics instructor Senda Berenson adapts Naismith's basketball rules for women and introduces the game to her students at Smith College.

1895: *November:* Mrs. Charles B. Brown wins the first U.S. women's amateur golf championship at Hempstead, New York. She finishes the 18-hole tournament in 132 strokes.
Also: Frances Willard publishes *A Wheel Within a Wheel,* her account of how she learned to ride a bicycle. It quickly becomes a best-seller.

1896: *April 4:* Teams from Stanford University and the University of California at Berkeley compete in the first women's college basketball game. Stanford wins 2–1.

1899: *September & October:* Rivals Jane C. Yatman and Jane Lindsay ride through the Long Island, New York, countryside setting long-distance bicycling records. First Yatman covers 700 miles in 81 hours, 5 minutes. Then Lindsay rides 800 miles in 91 hours, 48 minutes.

1900–1919: Pathfinders

1900: U.S. golfer Margaret Abbott becomes the first woman to win an Olympic gold medal, but her title is considered unofficial. Women's events wouldn't officially be added to the Olympics until 1912.

1901: *October 24:* Schoolteacher Annie Edson Taylor survives a 173-foot plunge over Niagara Falls in a wooden barrel. She is the first person ever to "shoot the Falls" and live. 📷

1904: Bertha Kapernick becomes the first woman to give a bronco riding exhibition at the Cheyenne, Wyoming, Frontier Days, the top rodeo in the United States. 📷

1905: Californian May Sutton, the youngest and best of four tennis-playing sisters, becomes the first American to win the women's singles title at Wimbledon.

1907: Annette Kellermann appears at Revere Beach in Boston, Massachusetts, in a one-piece bathing suit. She is one of the first women to wear such a suit in public. 📷

1909: *January 11:* Twelve women drive in an auto race from New York to Philadelphia and back. Four cars are forced out of the race due to various mishaps on the unpaved roads of Burlington, New Jersey, but five drivers complete the course to win prizes.

1910: *May 16:* Blanche Stuart Scott, 19, of Dayton, Ohio, begins the first solo auto trip across the country by a woman driver. Soon after she completes the trip, on September 2, she becomes the first female pilot to fly a plane solo.

1911: *July 8:* Nan Jane Aspinwall rides her bay mare into New York City, completing the first coast-to-coast horseback ride by a woman. She traveled the 3,000 miles from San Francisco in 301 days, including 193 days off for resting.

August 1: Harriet Quimby becomes the first woman in the United States and the second in the world to receive a pilot's license. 📷

1914: American Elizabeth "Bunny" Ryan pairs with Agnes Morton to win the first of her record 19 Wimbledon titles, all in doubles or mixed doubles.

1917: *March 17:* The first bowling tournament for women is held under the auspices of the Women's International Bowling Congress in St. Louis, Missouri.

August: Lucy Diggs Slowe wins the women's singles title at the first American Tennis Association (ATA) national tournament, becoming the first African American national female champion in any sport.

1920–1929: The Golden Age of Sports

1920: Ethelda Bleibtrey becomes the first American woman to win an official Olympic gold medal, setting a world record in the 100-meter freestyle swim. Soon afterward, 14-year-old American Aileen Riggin wins the gold in the springboard diving competition. 📷

1921: The manager of the Syracuse University men's baseball team hears that Goucher College has one of the best teams in the country and challenges them to a game. He rescinds the offer when he learns that Goucher is a women's college.

1922: Frustrated by the lack of international track-and-field competition for women, a French group holds the first of four Women's Olympic Games, featuring 11 track events including a 1,000-meter run. Athletes from the United States and six other countries compete in front of more than 2,000 fans.

1923: The Women's Division of the National Amateur Athletic Federation is organized to promote physical fitness among women and to protect women athletes from exploitation by promoters or other officials.

1926: *August 6:* Gertrude Ederle swims the English Channel in 14 hours, 31 minutes. Three weeks later, Mrs. Clemington Corson of New York takes an hour longer to make the trip. Disappointed at not being the first woman to make the swim, she notes that she is the first mother to do so. 📷

1928: *January 19:* Eleanora Sears wins the first U.S. women's squash racquets singles championship. 📷

1929: Ora Mae Washington wins her first ATA women's singles crown. She would win seven more through 1937. 📷
Also: Tuskegee Institute forms one of the first women's college track teams and adds women's events to its Tuskegee Relays track meet for the first time.

1930–1945: All-American Girls

1931: *January 10:* The girls' basketball team of the Magnolia A&M School in Monticello, Arkansas, beats the girls of Jonesboro Baptist, 143–1. Louise Hicks scores 69 points and Ruby Selph scores 53. In five games, Magnolia has scored a total of 455 points, versus 29 for their opponents.
November 8: The National Football League holds its first "Ladies' Day" at a game between the New York Giants and the Portsmouth Yellow Jackets.

1932: Mildred "Babe" Didrikson sets three world records in track and field and wins two gold medals and one silver at the Summer Olympics. 📷
Also: Two track athletes, Tidye Pickett and Louise Stokes, are the first African American women to win places on a U.S. Olympic team. Although both women would be replaced at the last moment, they would make the team again in 1936. 📷

193

1933: *October 7 & November 12:* On each of these days, jockey Judy Johnson wins three races against male jockeys.

November: Pope Pius XI condemns women who go to boxing matches, stating that it is not possible at boxing matches to preserve "the dignity and grace peculiar to women."

1935: *August 13:* Twenty thousand fans watch the first Roller Derby—basically a dance marathon on roller skates—at the Chicago Coliseum.

1940: *May 2:* Belle Martell of Van Nuys, California, officiates eight matches in San Bernardino, California, to become the first woman boxing referee.

1943: Philip K. Wrigley forms the All-American Girls Professional Baseball League with four teams, the Racine Belles, Rockford Peaches, Kenosha Comets, and South Bend Blue Sox. 📷

1944: Ann Curtis becomes the first woman—and the first swimmer—to win the James E. Sullivan Memorial Trophy, awarded every year since 1930 to the nation's top amateur athlete.

1946–1965: Ladies Through and Through

1948: *November & December:* Roller Derby enjoys a sudden burst of popularity when a series of matches are broadcast on television for the first time. 📷

Also: Alice Coachman becomes the first black woman to win an Olympic gold medal when she sets an Olympic record of 5 feet, 6⅛ inches in the high jump. 📷

1949: *May 29:* Wilson Sporting Goods agrees to sponsor the formation of the Ladies Professional Golf Association.

1950: Babe Didrikson wins $14,800 during the LPGA's first season, a record in women's golf for one year.

Also: Althea Gibson is the first African American to play in the United States Lawn Tennis Association's national championships at Forest Hills, New York.

1951: *September 11:* American Florence Chadwick, 32, becomes the first woman to swim the English Channel in both directions. She swam from France to England in 1950 and today becomes the first woman to swim from England to France, finishing in 16 hours, 22 minutes.

1952: *January 20:* Patricia McCormick becomes the first female bullfighter in North America, killing two bulls to great applause in Juarez, Mexico.

June 23: Organized baseball formally bans women when minor-league president George M. Trautman voids the contract that the Class B Harrisburg (Pennsylvania) Senators offer 24-year-old shortstop Eleanor Engle.

1953: *May 18:* Jacqueline Cochran becomes the first female pilot to break the sound barrier, flying at a speed of 652.337 miles per hour over the California desert.

Also: Toni Stone becomes the first woman to compete at the top level of the Negro baseball leagues when she spends the season playing second base for the Indianapolis Clowns. 📷

1954: *August 16:* The first issue of *Sports Illustrated* is published.

Also: After its twelfth season, the All-American Girls Professional Baseball League folds.

1956: *September 27:* Babe Didrikson, voted the Associated Press Female Athlete of the Half Century just six years earlier, dies of cancer at age 45.

Also: Diver Pat McCormick (not the bullfighter) wins Olympic gold medals in springboard and platform diving, a feat she also managed at the 1952 Olympics. She is voted the Associated Press outstanding female athlete of the year and becomes the second woman to win the Sullivan Trophy. Through 1956, American women have won the springboard gold at every Summer Olympics.

Also: Tenley Albright, 17, becomes the first American woman to win the gold medal in Olympic figure skating.

1957: Althea Gibson takes the women's singles crowns at both Wimbledon and Forest Hills. She is the first African American to win a title at either tournament. 📷

1960: *Summer:* Sprinter Wilma Rudolph becomes the first woman to win three track-and-field gold medals at one Olympics. 📷

1961: *February 15:* Golfer Louise Suggs beats 10 men to win a 54-hole invitational golf tournament.
February 15: On their way to the world figure-skating championships, 18 members of the United States Figure Skating Team die in a plane crash near Brussels, Belgium. Among the dead is 16-year-old female skating sensation Laurence Owen. At the time of the crash, Laurence is the reigning U.S. women's singles champion and the pairs champion, with her brother Dudley.
Also: Wilma Rudolph becomes the first African American woman to win the Sullivan Trophy. 📷

1964: *March 19:* Pilot Jerrie Mock, 38, takes off from Columbus, Ohio, in an attempt to become the first woman pilot to fly solo around the world. She succeeds on April 17, having covered 22,858.8 miles in 29 days with 21 stops along the way.

1966–1981: A New Era

1967: *April 19:* Kathrine Switzer, 20, enters the Boston Marathon under "K. Switzer" and finishes in 4 hours, 20 minutes. For the second year in a row, Roberta Gibb also runs the race, hiding in the bushes near the starting line and jumping into the pack once the runners begin. 📷

1969: *February 7:* Jockey Diane Crump rides Merre Indian at Hialeah to become the first woman to compete against men on a major U.S. flat track. 📷
February 22: Barbara Jo Rubin rides in and wins her first race at Charles Town, Virginia. She had been scheduled to ride in a race on January 15, but the horse's owner changed jockeys after her

male opponents threw rocks at her dressing room and threatened to boycott the race.

Also: Ruth White, 17, becomes the youngest national fencing champion and the first African American woman to win a major U.S. title.

1970: *May 2:* Diane Crump becomes the first female jockey to ride in the Kentucky Derby, astride Fathom. She finishes fifteenth in a field of 17.

1971: *September 2:* Cheryl White, 17, rides Jetolara to victory in the third race at Waterford Park in Chester, West Virginia. She is the first black female jockey in the United States to win a thoroughbred race.

1972: *April 17:* Nina Kuscsik, 33 and a mother of three, becomes the first official female finisher in the Boston Marathon. She breaks the tape ahead of 700 male runners and eight other women, including Kathrine Switzer, who is the third woman to finish.

June 23: President Richard M. Nixon signs Title IX of the 1972 Education Amendments into law, banning sex discrimination in schools receiving federal funds.

June 24: After a long legal battle, Bernice Gera, 41, umpires one minor-league game, between Geneva and Auburn in the Class A New York–Penn League. Then she quits, citing the physical and mental strain of fighting the baseball establishment.

Also: For the first time ever, *Sports Illustrated* chooses a Sports*woman* of the Year, Billie Jean King.

1973: *July 19:* The United States Tennis Association announces that women and men will earn equal prize money at the U.S. Open tennis championships.

September 20: Billie Jean King beats Bobby Riggs 6–4, 6–3, 6–3 in the "Battle of the Sexes." 📷

1974: *June:* The first issue of *womenSports* magazine is published. 📷

September 7: Little League national headquarters signs an order banning sex discrimination in its local chapters. 📷

1975: *August 3:* Karren Stead, 11, of Morrisville, Pennsylvania, becomes the first female to win the National Soap Box Derby.
Also: The Motor City Wheelers beat Southern Illinois University 26–9 to win the first National Women's Wheelchair Basketball Tournament.

1976: The International Women's Professional Softball Association is formed by Billie Jean King and a group of sports promoters. King and several other women athletes own the Connecticut Falcons team, which wins the first season's world series.
Also: Basketball is a medal sport for women at the Olympics for the first time. The United States team wins the silver medal while the Soviet Union takes home the gold.

1977: *January 4:* The Chicago White Sox hire Mary Shane as the first female TV play-by-play announcer in major-league baseball.
May 29: Janet Guthrie becomes the first woman to compete in the Indianapolis 500. She is forced to withdraw when her car develops mechanical difficulties after 27 laps. 📷
September 29: Eva Shain is the first woman to officiate a heavyweight championship fight, a match between Muhammad Ali and Ernie Shavers.

1978: *May 28:* Janet Guthrie is the first woman driver to complete the Indianapolis 500, finishing ninth against 33 men.
December 9: The Chicago Hustle beats the Milwaukee Does 92–87 in the first game played in the Women's Professional Basketball League (WBL). The league will last three seasons before folding.
Also: In a lawsuit brought by Melissa Ludtke of *Sports Illustrated*, a U.S. District Court judge rules that male and female reporters should have the same access to athletes, even if it means entering locker rooms while they're dressing.

1979: Billie Jean King surpasses Elizabeth "Bunny" Ryan when she wins her twentieth Wimbledon title. In all, she has collected six singles crowns, 10 doubles titles, and four mixed-doubles titles.

1980: The Women's Sports Foundation establishes the International

Women's Sports Hall of Fame. The first women inducted are golfer Patty Berg, Babe Didrikson, Amelia Earhart, Gertrude Ederle, Althea Gibson, Janet Guthrie, swimmer Eleanor Holm, Billie Jean King, and Wilma Rudolph.

1982–Today: Taut, Toned, and Coming On Strong

1982: *March 28:* Louisiana Tech beats Cheyney State 76–62, to win the first NCAA Division I national women's basketball championship.

1984: Coached by Pat Head Summitt of the University of Tennessee, the U.S. women's basketball team wins the gold medal at the Los Angeles Olympics. Players include Cheryl Miller, Anne Donovan, Lynette Woodard, and Teresa Edwards.

1985: *October 7:* The Harlem Globetrotters sign Lynette Woodard, former University of Kansas basketball star, as their first female player.
Also: Libby Riddles is the first woman ever to win the 1,100-mile Iditarod Trail Sled Dog Race in Alaska.

1986: Attorney and former Olympic rower Anita DeFrantz is appointed to a lifetime membership on the International Olympic Committee (IOC). DeFrantz is the first woman to represent the United States on the IOC, and is one of only five women on the 91-member committee.

1987: *February 4:* The first annual National Girls and Women in Sports Day is celebrated in the United States. The day, which aims to increase the visibility of female athletes and advance the struggle for equality in sports, is dedicated to the memory of Olympic volleyball great Flo Hyman.

1988: Julie Croteau is the first woman to play on a men's college baseball team when she takes the field for St. Mary's College of Maryland, an NCAA Division III school. She will go on to play for the Colorado Silver Bullets in 1994.

1989: *December:* Minor-league umpire Pam Postema leaves baseball after her contract is not renewed. She has served in the minor leagues for 13 seasons, six of them at the Triple-A level.

Also: After Susan Butcher wins the Iditarod in 1986, '87, and '88, the *Anchorage Times* names her the Sled Dog Racer of the Decade. 📷

1991: *January:* The NCAA elects Judith Sweet as its first female president.

May: Barbara Hedges is named athletic director for the University of Washington. She is the first female athletic director of an NCAA Division I school that plays football.

June 8: Julie Krone becomes the first female jockey to ride in the 123-year-old Belmont Stakes.

September 24: Twenty-year-old Canadian Manon Rheaume becomes the first woman to play for a National Hockey League team when she tends goal for the expansion Tampa Bay Lightning during an exhibition game. 📷

December: The United States defeats Norway to win the first women's World Cup soccer championship. 📷

1993: *October 30:* Erin Whitten becomes the first female ice-hockey goalie credited with a win in a minor-league game when she leads the Toledo (Ohio) Storm to a 6–5 victory over the Dayton (Ohio) Bombers in the East Coast Hockey League.

1994: *May 8:* The Colorado Silver Bullets begin their first season on Mother's Day, becoming the first professional women's baseball team since 1954. 📷

1995: *April 2:* The University of Connecticut Huskies women's basketball team ends a perfect 35–0 season by beating the University of Tennessee Lady Volunteers in the final round of the NCAA Division I championships. 📷

July 14: New Jersey's Rutgers University hires C. Vivian Stringer as its women's basketball coach for an annual base salary of $150,000. Stringer, who compiled a record of 269–84 in 12 seasons at the University of Iowa, will earn $5,000 more than the men's football coach and $26,000 more than the men's basketball coach.

July 24: Veteran radio sports reporter Suzyn Waldman becomes the first woman to call a major-league baseball game for a TV broadcast network when she is in the booth for a New York Yankees–Texas Rangers game on ABC.

1996: Women's soccer and women's softball become medal sports at the Summer Olympics for the first time.

1998: *February:* At the Winter Olympics in Nagano, Japan, women's ice hockey becomes a medal sport for the first time.

RESOURCES

Resources on women in sports used to be as scarce as women's athletic events on TV. Fortunately, both are becoming easier to find. Biographies written for young-adult audiences are available on a great number of female daredevils and athletes, from Bessie Coleman and Babe Didrikson to Martina Navratilova and Jackie Joyner-Kersee. In addition, the books, videotapes, and organizations listed here address some of the topics discussed in this book. Where appropriate, the intended audience of a book is identified as adult or young adult. Those books without such designations are adult volumes that are particularly accessible to a younger audience.

On Sports, Gender, and Related Issues

Aaseng, Nathan. *The Locker Room Mirror: How Sports Reflect Society.* New York: Walker and Company, 1993. This thought-provoking young-adult book looks at how the sports world responds to and is affected by drugs, violence, cheating, racial discrimination, sex discrimination, and the influence of money.

Cahn, Susan K. *Coming On Strong: Gender and Sexuality in Twentieth-Century Women's Sport.* New York: The Free Press, 1994. Written for an adult audience, this is a powerful, valuable study that examines the social issues and controversies that have shaped women's sports over the last 100 years.

Cayleff, Susan E. *Babe: The Life and Legend of Babe Didrikson Zaharias.* Urbana, Illinois: University of Illinois Press, 1995. Painstakingly researched, this adult book is at once a detailed biography of an extraordinary athlete and an insightful social history of twentieth-century America.

Macy, Sue. *A Whole New Ball Game: The Story of the All-American Girls Professional Baseball League.* New York: Henry Holt, 1993. Written for young adults, this book uses interviews, photographs, and material from players' scrapbooks to follow the rise and fall of the pioneering league and look at the players' lives both on and off the field.

Nelson, Mariah Burton. *Are We Winning Yet? How Women Are Changing Sports and Sports Are Changing Women.* New York: Random House, 1991. Nelson talks to female athletes and sports fans in the process of exploring a number of the issues that define the changing landscape of American women's sports.

Nelson, Mariah Burton. *The Stronger Women Get, the More Men Love Football: Sexism and the American Culture of Sports.* New York: Harcourt Brace & Company, 1994. This adult book is a compelling, personal study of how sports have influenced and continue to influence attitudes about gender in American culture.

Ryan, Joan. *Little Girls in Pretty Boxes: The Making and Breaking of Elite Gymnasts and Figure Skaters.* New York: Doubleday, 1995. Ryan exposes the underside of two sports in which girls with dreams of glory too often pay the price by developing eating disorders and suffering permanent, even life-threatening injuries.

Excellent Reference Sources

Gregorich, Barbara. *Women at Play: The Story of Women in Baseball.* New York: Harcourt Brace & Company, 1993. This is a lively overview of the part women have played in the history of America's national pastime, with up-close-and-personal features on many outstanding ball players.

Hult, Joan S., and Marianna Trekell, editors. *A Century of Women's Basketball: From Frailty to Final Four.* Reston, Virginia: American Alliance for Health, Physical Education, Recreation and Dance, 1991. Many of the essays in this adult-level history of women's basketball were written by the female coaches and athletic directors who shaped the game.

Sherr, Lynn, and Jurate Kazickas. *Susan B. Anthony Slept Here: A Guide to American Women's Landmarks.* New York: Times Books, 1994. This guidebook brings women's history to life by pointing out museums, monuments, and landmarks dedicated to women throughout the 50 states. Among the athletes featured are mountain-climber Dora Keen, who has a mountain range named for her in Alaska; all-around star Babe Didrikson, honored with a museum in Texas; and Frances Willard, whose bicycle, Gladys, is on display in her Illinois museum.

Woolum, Janet. *Outstanding Women Athletes: Who They Are and How They Influenced Sports in America.* Phoenix, Arizona: Oryx Press, 1992. A valuable reference, this book combines biographical sketches of 60 important athletes with an excellent historical overview of American women in sports and a summary of the women's highlights from each of the Summer and Winter Olympic Games.

On African American Athletes

Ashe, Arthur R., Jr. *A Hard Road to Glory: A History of the African-American Athlete.* New York: Amistad Press, Inc., 1988. This three-volume set offers a comprehensive account of the accomplishments of African American male athletes from 1619 to 1988, with spottier but still valuable material on women's sports and specific women athletes.

Black Women in Sport Foundation, producer. *Amazing Grace: Black Women in Sport,* 1993. This 25-minute video, narrated by broadcaster Robin Roberts, focuses on the achievements of African American women athletes, coaches, and sports administrators from the 1950s through the early 1990s. Available from the Black Women in Sport Foundation (see address below).

Davis, Michael D. *Black American Women in Olympic Track and Field: A Complete Illustrated Reference.* Jefferson, North Carolina: McFarland & Company, 1992. This notable resource includes a comprehensive listing of every female African American Olympic track athlete through 1992, along with a biographical sketch of each woman.

On Homophobia in Sports

Mosbacher, Dee, producer. *Out for a Change: Addressing Homophobia in Women's Sports,* 1995. This 27-minute video tackles the issue of homophobia by interviewing athletes and following the progress of a workshop in which college teammates work through their attitudes about lesbians in sports. An accompanying curriculum guide was developed by Professor Pat Griffin of the University of Massachusetts, Amherst. Available from Woman Vision c/o Transit Media, 22D Hollywood Avenue, Hohokus, NJ 07423; phone 1-800-343-5540.

Young, Perry Deane. *Lesbians and Gays in Sports.* New York: Chelsea House, 1995. Written for young adults, this book addresses homophobia in sports and looks at the experiences of lesbian and gay male athletes who have come out of the closet.

Great Sports Reporting

Blais, Madeleine. *In These Girls, Hope Is a Muscle.* New York: The Atlantic Monthly Press, 1995. Expanded from an article in *The New York Times Magazine,* this book takes an intimate look at one championship season with the Lady Hurricanes girls' high-school basketball team of Amherst, Massachusetts.

Rapoport, Ron, editor. *A Kind of Grace: A Treasury of Sportswriting by Women.* Berkeley, California: Zenobia Press, 1994. From Betty Cuniberti's heartbreaking account of golfer Heather Farr's battle against cancer to Melissa Isaacson's gentle tribute to the tenacity of basketball-player Nancy Lieberman, this diverse collection of articles captures the excitement and poignancy of women's sports.

womenSports, 1974–1978. The first five years of the magazine that Billie Jean King started in 1974 offer the single best chronicle of the athletes, issues, and events that were important during the 1970s revolution in women's sports. The most memorable issue of all was the August 1977 focus on tomboys, complete with a "Tomboy Who's Who" of famous women who were tomboys growing up and an article on the sports played by the First Ladies of the United States.

Organizations

Black Women in Sport Foundation, P.O. Box 2610, Philadelphia, Pennsylvania 19130; phone 215-763-6609; fax 215-763-2855. This nonprofit organization, established in 1992, aims to increase the participation of African American girls and women in recreational sports and sports careers. The foundation develops educational materials, runs coaching clinics, awards scholarships, and sponsors a mentor program that pairs African American girls with adult role models.

Melpomene Institute, 1010 University Avenue, St. Paul, Minnesota 55104; phone 612-642-1951; fax 612-642-1871. Founded in 1982, this nonprofit organization conducts research and publishes materials on women's health and physical activity. Melpomene (pronounced mel-POM-uh-nee) also publishes books, brochures, and journals and produces videos on girls and women in sports.

National Women's History Project, 7738 Bell Road, Windsor, California 95492-8518; phone 707-838-6000; fax 707-838-0478. This nonprofit educational organization, started in 1980, publishes posters and other women's history materials, conducts teacher-training workshops, and sells women's history books, videos, posters, and CD-ROM software through a mail-order catalog. The catalog contains biographies of women athletes and other material on women in sports.

Women's Sports Foundation, Eisenhower Park, East Meadow, New York 11554; phone 1-800-227-3988; fax 516-542-4716. Established in 1974, this nonprofit organization promotes and enhances sports and fitness opportunities for girls and women by providing grants to athletes, fighting to protect Title IX, and working to influence sports policy in other ways. The 800 number also is the foundation's Infoline, which people are welcome to call with questions about women's sports.

INDEX

(Page numbers in *italic* refer to illustrations.)

Abbott, Margaret, 191
ABC, 167
Advertisements, *19, 31, 47, 64,*
    70, *185*
African American women,
    43–45, *44, 71,* 105–10, *123,*
    197
    in baseball, 99–106, *101,* 195
    first on Olympic team, 86–87,
        87, 193
    in tennis, 44, 45, 60–62, *61,*
        107–10, *111, 124,* 192, 193,
        194, 196
    in track and field, 84–87, *85,*
        87, 106–7, *107, 108,* 150,
        156, *158, 175,* 194, 196
Air Force, U.S., 169–70
Akers, Michelle, *164*
Albright, Tenley, 195
All-American Girls Professional
    Baseball League, 90–94,
    91, 105, *106,* 169, 194, 195

All-American Girls Softball
    League, 90
Amateur Athletic Union (AAU),
    63–65, 70, 84, 87, 132
    1930 track-and-field champi-
        onships of, 78–81
Amateur Softball Association,
    89
Amdur, Neil, 129
American Farmer, 17, 20
American Physical Education
    Association (APEA), 41
American Tennis Association
    (ATA), 45, 60–62, 192, 193
America's Cup, *177*
Anderson, Ada, 24–25, *26,* 189
Anthony, Susan B., 28
Archery, 23, *24,* 190
"Are Athletics Making Girls
    Masculine?" (Sargent),
    42–43
Ashford, Evelyn, *175*

Aspinwall, Nan Jane, 192
Association for Intercollegiate
    Athletics for Women
    (AIAW), 130, 136, 154
Athletic scholarships, 135, 136
Aviation, *38*, 38–39, *71*, 191, 192,
    195, 196

Barnett, Marilyn, 142
Baseball, 12, *93*, 138, 190, 192,
    195
    African American women in,
        99–106, *101*, 195
    Little League, 132–34, *133*,
        197
    major-league, women
        announcers in, 198, 201
    men's, women playing in, *75*,
        98, 99–102, *101*, 103–5,
        106, 195, 199
    women coaches in, 200–201
    women's professional, 89–94,
        91, 105, *106*, *168*, 169–70,
        194, 195, 199, 200
    women umpires in, 197, 200
Basketball, 14, 22, 28–30, *29*, *41*,
    42, 43, 44, *44*, 63, 80, 103,
    136–38, *137*, 166–67, 179,
    184–86, 190, 193, 198, 199
    1995 NCAA championships,
        151–54, *153*, 166–67, 200
    standardization of rules for,
        40–42
Bayard, Ferdinand, 20
Beauty ideal, 155
Beecher, Catharine, 12, 20–22,
    21, 189
Benoit, Joan, *173*

Berenson, Senda, 28, 40, 43, 190
Berg, Patty, 199
Beringer, Minnie, *73*
Berkow, Ira, 187
Berlage, Gai Ingham, 188
Berube, Carla, *153*
Bicycles, 15–16, *17*, 27–28, *31*, 36,
    190, 191
Blackburn, Mt., 36
Blair, Bonnie, *176*
Blatt, Genevieve, 134
Bleibtrey, Ethelda, 192
Blonde Comet, The, 94
Bloomer, Amelia, 27
Bloomers, 27
Body building, 97
Boston Marathon, 12, 130–32,
    131, 196, 197
Boston Post, 39
Bowling, *73*, 88, 192
Boxing, *49*, *82*, *145*, 178
    women referees in, 194, 198
Bras, for sports, 157–59
Brasuhn, Toughie, *117*
Brewer, Relna, 97
Bromo Quinine, *64*
Bronco riding, *76*, 191
Brooks running shoes, 159
Brough, Louise, 107–9, 110
Brown, Earlene, 119
Brown, Mrs. Charles B., 190
Brundage, Avery, 83
Bryn Mawr College, *32*, 40
Bullfighting, 195
Business world, athletics and,
    187–88
Butcher, Susan, 160–61, *161*, 199,
    200

California Eagle, 84
Calisthenics, 20–21, *21, 22, 77*
Carroll, Kathy, 166–67
CBS, 117, 138, 152, 187
Century Illustrated Monthly Magazine, 40
Chadwick, Florence, 195
Chambers, Dorothy Lambert, 57–58
Champion's Choice (Tunis), 94
Chapman, Betty, *123*
Cheerleaders, 103, *104*
Chicago Defender, 60–62, 86
Childbirth, 42
Clothing
    designed specifically for sports, 157–59
    increased comfort in, 27–28, 36
    in nineteenth century, 18–20, *19, 23, 26,* 27–28
    in 1920s, *54,* 55
    one-piece bathing suit, *47,* 191
    for tennis, *26,* 27, *57, 58*
Coaching, 178, 179, 200–201
Coachman, Alice, 106, *107,* 194
Cochran, Jacqueline, 195
Coleman, Bessie, *71*
College sports, 22, 28–30, 40–43, *41,* 45, 63, 65–66, 138, *153,* 166, 179, 190, 192, 193
    African American women in, 44, 84, 87
    increased interest in, 151–55
    reversal of restrictive policy on, 130, 134
    standardization of rules for, 40–42

Title IX and, 134–36, 154, 197
    see also Women's colleges
Collier's, 82, *93*
Collins, Dottie Wiltse, *91,* 92
Colorado Silver Bullets, *168,* 169–70, 199, 200
Committee on Women's Athletics (CWA), 41
Company-sponsored teams, 63, 78–80
Competition
    first between sexes, 189
    first for women on national level, 23
    limited by Women's Division, 62–66
    supposed ill effects of, 43
Congress, U.S., 134–36
Cook, Bell, 190
Cooley's, *19*
Coolidge, Calvin, 53
Copeland, Lillian, *96*
Corliss, Richard, 155
Corporate sponsors, 184–87
Corsets, 18–20, *19, 26,* 27
Corson, Mrs. Clemington, 193
Cosmopolitan, 27–28
Court, Margaret Smith, 125–26
Cowgirls, *76,* 190, 191
Croquet, 22–23, *23*
Croteau, Julie, 199
Crump, Diane, *149,* 196, 197
Curtis, Ann, 194

Daily News (London), 51
Dancer, Faye, *106*
Daredevils, 33–39, *34,* 191, 45
Davis, Cathy "Cat," *145*

Deford, Frank, 119
DeFrantz, Anita, 199
de Koven, Anna, 27–28, 36
Depression, Great, 83, 87–88
Didrikson, Mildred "Babe," 3, 4,
    78–83, 79, 82, 83, 89, 113,
    115, 193, 194, 195, 199
Diving, 47, 72, 192, 195
Doering, Uschi, 145
Dogsled racing, 160–61, 161,
    199, 200
Dyer, Kelly, 162

Earhart, Amelia, 3, 4, 199
Ederle, Gertrude, 51–53, 52, 56,
    57, 70, 191, 199
Education Amendments (1972),
    Title IX of, 134–36, 154,
    197
Eisen, Gail, 155
Eleneki, Mahina, 171
Endorsements, 142–43
Engle, Eleanor, 195
English Channel
    first woman to fly across, 38
    swimming across, 51–53, 52,
    56, 57, 191, 195
Equipment, designed specifi-
    cally for women, 157–59,
    169, 178, 179
ESPN, 152, 167
Evans, Janet, 174
Evert, Chris, 143, 156, 157, 181

Fallows, Alice Katharine, 40
Femininity issue, 42, 83, 90–94,
    100–103, 139–41, 159, 187
Fencing, 44, 197

Field hockey, 22, 41, 44
Figure skating, 95, 103, 144, 172,
    195, 196
Fitness phenomenon, 155
Fleming, Peggy, 144
Flying. See Aviation
Football, 138, 193, 199
Fox hunts, 20
Fraser, Gretchen, 121

Gayton, Zoe, 190
Gehrig, Lou, 12
Gera, Bernice, 197
Gibb, Roberta, 196
Gibson, Althea, 6–7, 8, 107–10,
    111, 124, 194, 196, 199
Gilbert, Bil, 178
Glamour, 156–57
Goboess, Delilah, 189
Godey's Lady's Book, 20, 23
Golf, 74, 82, 110–16, 113, 120,
    148, 190, 191, 194, 196
    sexuality issue and, 141,
    184–87
Good Housekeeping, 36, 39
Goodnough, Abby, 166
Goucher College, 32, 192
Gould, Jack, 105
Green, Dallas, 133
Guthrie, Janet, 147, 198, 199
Gymnastics, 12, 30, 44, 63, 103,
    155, 156

Harper's Monthly Magazine, 65
Harper's Weekly, 17–18
Hedges, Barbara, 200
Helmbreck, Valerie, 184–87
Henie, Sonja, 95

Hepburn, Katharine, *113, 114,*
    115–16
Hicks, Betty, 112–15
Hicks, Louise, 193
High jump, 106, *107,* 194
High-school sports, 29, 63, 65,
    138, 162
    Title IX and, 134–36, 197
Hitler, Adolf, 86
Holm, Eleanor, 199
Homophobia, 141–43, 184–87
Hoover, Lou Henry, 63
Horseback riding, 17, 20, 190, 192
    rodeos and, *76,* 191
Horse racing, 20, *149,* 194,
    196–97, 200
Howell, Mrs. M. C., 190

Ice hockey, 161–62, *162,* 178–79,
    200, 201
Ice skating, 17–18, *176*
    see also Figure skating
Iditarod Trail Sled Dog Race,
    160–61, *161,* 199, 200
Indianapolis 500, *147,* 198
International Olympic Commit-
    tee (IOC), 68, 199
International Women's Sports
    Hall of Fame, 198–99

Javelin toss, *79,* 80
Jazz Age, 53–55, *54*
Jefferson, Linda, 138
Jet, 100–102
Jewett, Emma, 190
Jockeys, *149,* 194, 196–97, 200
JogBra, 157–59
Jogging, 182

Johnson, Dana, *153*
Johnson, Judy, 194
Jonesboro Baptist, 193
Joyce, Joan, *146*
Joyner-Kersee, Jackie, 155,
    156–57, *158*

Kapernick, Bertha, 191
Keen, Dora, 36
Kellerman, Annette, *47,* 191
Kellogg's Pep Bran Flakes, *64*
Kentucky Derby, 197
Kerrigan, Nancy, 165
King, Billie Jean, 125–29, *127,*
    128, 139, 142–43, 187, 197,
    198, 199
King, Carolyn, 133
Kirsky, George, 80
Krone, Julie, 200
Kuscsik, Nina, 197

"Ladies' Days," 190, 193
Ladies Home Journal, 42–43, 103
Ladies' Indispensable Assistant,
    The, 18
Ladies Professional Golf Associ-
    ation (LPGA), 112–15,
    187, 194
League of Their Own, A, 169
Lenglen, Suzanne, 56–60, *59, 62*
Lesbianism, 141–43, 184–87
Levette, Harry, 84
Liberty, 93
Lieberman-Cline, Nancy, 152,
    154
Lindsay, Jane, 191
Little League, 132–34, *133,* 197
Lobo, Rebecca, *186*

Lopez, Nancy, *148*
Lopiano, Donna, 160
Ludtke, Melissa, 138, 198

McAboy, Cassandra, 165–66
McCombs, M. J., 80
McCormick, Pat (diver), 195
McCormick, Patricia (bull-
      fighter), 195
McGeehan, W. O., 51
Madison Square Garden,
      Navratilova banner at,
      10–12, *13*
Magnolia A&M School, 193
Marathons, 12, 130–32, *131, 173,*
      196, 197
Marathon walking, 23–26, 70,
      189, 190
Marble, Alice, 115
Marciniak, Michelle, *153*
Marshall, Mary, 189
Marshall, Penny, 169
Martell, Belle, 194
Media, *140,* 152, 163–67, 179
   in Golden Age of Sports
      Reporting (1920s), 55–56,
      70
   "ladylike" qualities of
      women athletes stressed
      by, 92–94
   spotty coverage of women's
      sports in, 138–39, 163–65
   see also specific publications
Meek, Carrie, 187–88
Menstruation, 42
Meyers, Ann, 136–38, *137,* 154
Mighty Mary, 177
Miller, Hinda, 157–59

Miranda, Francisco de, 20
Mitchell, Virne Beatrice
      "Jackie," 12, *98*
Mock, Jerrie, 196
Moran, Gussie, 115
Morton, Agnes, 192
Motherhood, 18, 42
Mountain climbing, 36
Ms., 159–60
Murray, Arthur, 105

Naismith, James, 28, 190
National Amateur Athletic Fed-
      eration (NAAF), Women's
      Division of, 63–66, 70, 92,
      103, 130, 134, 193
National Archery Champi-
      onship, 23, 190
National Baseball Hall of Fame,
      169
National Collegiate Athletic
      Association (NCAA),
      135–36, 151–54, *153,* 163,
      166, 179, 199, 200
National Enquirer, 142
National Soap Box Derby, 198
National Training School for
      Women and Girls, *44*
Navratilova, Martina, 10–12, *13,*
      14, 142, 155–56, *157*
NBC, 138
Nelson, Mariah Burton, 165
New Deal, 88
New Woman, 36–37, *37,* 39, 46
New York Daily News, 55
New York Herald-Tribune, 51
New York Times, 25, 53, 56, 105,
      128, 129, 160, 165, 166, 187

"Next to Marriage, We'll Take Golf" (Hicks), 112–15
Niagara Falls, 33–35, *34*, 191
Niekro, Joe, 170
Nike, *185*
Norris, J. Anna, 42

Oakley, Annie, 190
Official Basket Ball Guide for Women, 42
Officiating, 194, 197, 198, 200
Olympic Games, 14, 30, 63, 162, 163, 195, 201
    concern over women's track-and-field events at, 66–68, *67*
    first African American women sent to, 86–87, *87*, 193
    first Americans to win medals in, 191, 192
    1928, 66–68, *67*, 81
    1932, 78, *79*, 81, 82, 86, 193
    1936, 86, *87*
    1948, 106, *107, 121*, 194
    1960, 106–7, *108*, 119, 129, 196
    1976, 138, 198
    1984, 155, *156, 173, 175*, 199
    1988, 156, *174*
    1992, 156, *172*
    1994, *176*
O'Neill, Peggy, *75*
One-piece bathing suit, *47*, 191
Outerbridge, Mary, 26–27, 189
Owen, Laurence, 196
Owens, Jesse, 86–87

Paige, Satchel, 99–100
Passion to Play, A, 167
Pat and Mike, 113, 114, 115–16
Payne, Monta Jean, *117*
Peanuts, 139
Pedestrianism. *See* Marathon walking
Pepe, Maria, 132–33, *133*
Petticoats, 18–20, *26*
Physical Education, 18
Physical education programs, 22, *32*, 62–66
Physiology and Calisthenics (Beecher), 21, *21*, 189
Pickett, Tidye, 84, *85*, 86, *87*, 106, 193
Pierce, Mary, 165
Pius XI, Pope, 194
Play-by-play announcers, 198, 199, 201
Poole, Sharon, 132, 133
Postema, Pam, 200
Prentice, Jo Ann, 141
Prize money, 125, 179, 197

Quimby, Harriet, *38*, 38–39, 45, 192

Race car driving, *147*, 191, 198
Radke, Lina, *67*
Rawls, Betsy, 112–15
Retton, Mary Lou, 155, *156*
Rheaume, Manon, 162, *162*, 200
Rice, Grantland, 58, 81–82
Riddles, Libby, 161, 199
Riggin, Aileen, *72*, 192
Riggs, Bobby, 125–29, *127*, 197
Riggs, Phyllis, *104*

Road Runners Club of America, 182

Roaring Twenties, 53–55, *54*

Robinson, Jackie, *124*

Rodeos, *76*, 191

Role models, 166–69

Roller Derby, 116–20, *117, 118,* 194

Roosevelt, Franklin, 87, 90

Rowing, 30

Rubin, Barbara Jo, 196

Rudolph, Wilma, 106–7, *108,* 130, 196, 199

Running, 44
    safety issues and, 182–84
    see also Track and field

Running shoes, 159

Rush, Wendi, *171*

Ruth, Babe, 12

Ryan, Elizabeth "Bunny," 192, 198

Ryan, Linda Truman, 165, 166

Sabatini, Gabriela, 10–11

Safety (bicycle), 27

Safety issues, 179–84

San Francisco Examiner, 29

Sargent, Dudley A., 42–43

Satriano, Gina, *168*

Saturday Evening Post, 58, 92–94, 112–15

Scholarships, 135, 136

Schroder, Frank C., 92

Schulz, Charles, *139*

Scott, Blanche Stuart, 191

Sears, Eleanora Randolph, 68–70, *69,* 193

Seles, Monica, 165

Self-image, 159–60

Selph, Ruby, 193

Seltzer, Jerry, 119

Seltzer, Leo, 116, 119

Shain, Eva, 198

Shane, Mary, 198

Shiley, Jean, 81

Shot put, *96*

Sierens, Gayle, 199

Skiing, *121*

Slowe, Lucy Diggs, 45, 107, 192

Smith College, 12–14, 28, *32,* 40, 190

Soccer, 41, 163, *164, 182, 183,* 188, 200, 201

Softball, *88,* 88–90, 105, 119, *123, 146,* 198

Spalding Sports, 169

Speed skating, *176*

Sporting News, 152

Sports clubs, 44

Sports Illustrated, 104, 138, 141, 143, 165, 166, 178, 195, 197, 198

Sports reporting, 55–56, 70, 165–66
    access to locker rooms and, 138
    see also Media

Squash, 68, 193

Stanford University, 29, 190

Stead, Karren, 198

Stephans, Lydia, 167

Stokes, Louise, 84, 86, *87,* 106, 193

Stone, Toni, 99–106, *101,* 195

Stormer bicycles, *31*

Street, Gabby, 100

Stringer, C. Vivian, 200–201

Suffrage, 46
Suggs, Louise, 196
James E. Sullivan Memorial Trophy, 194, 195, 196
Summit, Pat Head, 199
Supreme Court, U.S., 136
Sutton, May, 191
Sweet, Judith, 200
Swimming, 41, 44, *47*, 63, *122, 174*, 189, 192, 194
    across English Channel, 51–53, *52*, 56, *57*, 191, 195
Switzer, Kathrine, 130–32, *131*, 196, 197
Swoopes, Sheryl, *185*

Taylor, Annie Edson, 33–35, *34, 35*, 45, 191
Team sports, 39–43, 45–46
    concern over effects of, 41–43
    introduced to women, 22
    see also specific sports
Television, 138, 152, 163–65, 167
    Roller Derby and, 116–19
Tennis, 10–12, *13*, 26–27, *50, 83*, 120, 138, 155–56, *157, 180, 181*, 189, 191, 192, 197, 198
    African American women in, 44, 45, 60–62, *61*, 107–10, *111, 124*, 192, 193, 194, 196
    clothing for, *26*, 27, 57, 58
    Lenglen-Wills rivalry and, 56–60, *59, 62*
    and Riggs's challenges to women players, 125–29, *127, 128*, 197
    sexuality issue and, 142–43
Time, 89, 155

Title IX, 134–36, 154, 197
Track and field, 14, 40, 41, 63, 78–87, *79, 83, 96*, 119, 192, 193
    African American women in, 84–87, *85, 87*, 106–7, *107, 108*, 150, 156, *158, 175*, 194, 196
    and concern over Olympic events, 66–68, *67*
    marathons, 12, 130–32, *131*, 196, 197, *173*
    negative depictions of women in, 82–84
Tracy, Spencer, *114*, 115
Trap-shooting, *48*
"Truth About Women Athletes, The," 100–102
Tunis, John, 63–68, 94
Tuskegee Institute, 14, 84, 87, 193
Tyus, Wyomia, *150*

Umpires, 197, 200
United States (Lawn) Tennis Association, 45, 197
United States tennis championships, 58, 60, 107–9, 110, *157*, 194, 196, 197
University of California at Berkeley, 29–30, 190
University of Connecticut Huskies, 151–52, *153*, 166, *186*, 200

Vare, Glenna Collett, *74*
Vassar, Matthew, 22
Vassar College, 22, *32*, 40, *41*, 43

INDEX

Virginia Slims tour, 10–11, 126
Volleyball, 22, *171*
Voting rights, 46

Waldman, Suzyn, 201
Walking, 17
  marathon, 23–26, 70, 189,
    190
Washington, Ora Mae, 12,
    60–62, *61*, 70, 107, 193
Wellesley College, 22, 30, *32*
Wenzell, Marge, *106*
Weston, Joanie, 119
White, Cheryl, 197
White, Ruth, 197
Whitten, Erin, 161–62, 200
Willard, Frances, 15–16, *17*, 27,
    188, 190
William Morris Agency, 53
Williams, Esther, *122*
Williamson, Nancy, 178
Wills, Helen, 56–57, 58–60, *59*,
    62, *62*, 70
Wilson Sporting Goods, 194
Wimbledon, 57–58, 60, 109, 110,
    111, 138, 142–43, 191, 192,
    196, 198
"Women and the Sport Busi-
    ness" (Tunis), 65
Women's Basketball Rules Com-
    mittee, 40
Women's colleges, 37, 44, 193
  physical education programs
    at, 22, *32*

team sports at, 28–30, 39–43,
    45
Women's Division, 63–66, 70, 92,
    103, 130, 134, 193
Women's International Bowling
    Congress, *73*, 192
Women's Olympic Games, 192
womenSports, 138, 139, *140*, 197
Women's Professional Basket-
    ball League (WBL), 198
Women's Professional Golfers
    Association (WPGA),
    110–12
Women's Sports and Fitness, 160
Woodard, Lynette, 199
Works Progress Administration
    (WPA), 88
World Cup soccer, 163, *164*, *183*,
    200
World War I, 46
World War II, 90, 92
  women's role at end of,
    102–3
Wright, Ben, 184–87
Wrigley, Philip K., 89–94, 194

Yacht-racing, *177*
Yamaguchi, Kristi, *172*
Yatman, Jane C., 191
Yoder, Robert, 92
Young Men's Christian Associa-
    tion (YMCA), 18, 44
Young Women's Christian Asso-
    ciation (YWCA), 44

DATE DUE

MAR 1 7 2003			
MAY R 2004			
JAN - 4 2006			

Demco, Inc. 38-293